MILTON

AND THE LITERATURE OF TRAVEL

PRINCETON STUDIES IN ENGLISH, NO. 32

MILTON
and the Literature of Travel

BY ROBERT RALSON CAWLEY

PRINCETON, NEW JERSEY

PRINCETON UNIVERSITY PRESS

1951

PRINTED IN THE UNITED STATES OF AMERICA
BY PRINCETON UNIVERSITY PRESS AT PRINCETON, NEW JERSEY

TO MY BROTHER
Charles James Cawley

PREFACE

SOME years ago when I was investigating the relation between travel literature and the Elizabethan drama I became interested in the influence of that same literature on Milton. It was clear that geography was so dominant an element with the poet that a separate study should be devoted to him alone. Professor Allan Gilbert's *Geographical Dictionary* was already in the field, with its significant statement: "In the poetry of Milton geography is rivaled in importance by none of the sciences except astronomy." When, years later, I asked Professor Gilbert whether he intended to write a companion volume drawing conclusions based on the *Dictionary*, he told me that other projects had intervened and that he would gladly release the subject to me.

The present study is, therefore, an attempt to show how Milton used the travel literature in his poetry, which among the travel books were his favorites, how he adapted their materials to his poetic purposes, and how his lines were enriched by the abundant and colorful details provided by those books.

I have omitted Europe because travel on that continent falls into another category—except for Russia, which, in Milton's day, was apt to be thought of as part of Asia. Another liberty I have taken is to extend the use of "traveler" to include "writer of travels."

I wish here to acknowledge my debt to Professor Gilbert's *Dictionary* and to E. H. Sugden's *Topographical Dictionary to the Works of Shakespeare and his Fellow Dramatists.* I have found both books of inestimable value in checking my own research. On the more personal side I am glad to record my gratitude to Mr. A. I. Ellis of the British Museum, where most of this book was written. Finally, I owe most

Preface

of all to my wife, who has helped in a thousand ways to make the work possible.

ROBERT R. CAWLEY

Princeton, N.J.
January 22, 1951

CONTENTS

PREFACE   vii

INTRODUCTION   3

CHAPTER I. MILTON'S POETIC ADAPTATION
    OF GEOGRAPHY   9

CHAPTER II. FURTHER CHARACTERISTIC USES
    OF GEOGRAPHIC MATERIAL   24

CHAPTER III. MILTON AND RUSSIA   42

CHAPTER IV. MILTON'S TRADITIONALISM   65

CHAPTER V. A GROWING CONSCIENCE   84

CHAPTER VI. ANCIENT AND MODERN   116

CONCLUSION   139

BIBLIOGRAPHY   142

INDEX   149

MILTON

AND THE LITERATURE OF TRAVEL

INTRODUCTION

THE study of Geography is both profitable and delightfull." Thus wrote Milton in his Preface to *A Brief History of Moscovia*. From early days, it is clear, geography was an important part of his curriculum, and it therefore finds a place in his own tract on education, where he advises the pupil "to learn in any modern Author, the use of the Globes, and all the Maps; first with the old names, and then with the new." And even after he went blind we find him inquiring from a traveling friend which is the best and most up-to-date atlas: "In the matter of the Atlas you have abundantly performed all I requested of you. . . . Be good enough, pray, to take so much farther trouble for me as to be able to inform me, when you return, how many volumes there are in the complete work, and which of the two issues, that of Blaeu or that of Jansen, is the larger and more correct." The most significant statement here is the last one, his insistence on the "more correct." The very undertaking of his project for writing a history of Russia carries its own meaning. He will, as he says, attempt to set "a Pattern or Example" of how other geographies might be written by digesting other men's too voluminous accounts and by using, so far as possible, only the evidence as presented by eyewitnesses. Certainly he has in this little work succeeded in saving the reader from the weary travel of moving through so many "desert Authours."

An interest so deep and real as this would be sure to leave its mark on Milton's poetry. A sensitive mind like his would recognize at once the value of imaginative material furnished by the great voyaging tradition. New information supplied by travelers of the previous hundred years, old information revitalized by new experience would provide enrichment for his mature poetry. Men were learning more all the time about the far eastern lands, India and China, about Africa

3

and Egypt, about the Holy Land, even about that strange, vast continent of America. Then, as if to start the new century out right, Hakluyt had poured forth his profound contributions just in time for authors of the 1600's to make full use of them. And Milton fell heir to these incomparable riches. Many a passage in *Paradise Lost* gains substance and meaning because writers like Hakluyt had added immeasurably to what Englishmen of the time knew about foreign countries. Naturally Milton depended on his "fit audience" to have that knowledge. And naturally too he used it to give body and background to much of what he had to say. Some of his finest lines depend for their power on this very objectification. Thus Satan's hunt for the serpent acquires special significance when the reader can visualize his having gone even,

> to the Ocean barr'd
> At *Darien*.

Or, clearly, the first garments of Adam and Eve take on more reality when the tree from which they are made is compared to,

> such as at this day to *Indians* known
> In *Malabar* or *Decan*.

The skillful adaptation of these materials to his purpose adds greatly to the stature of Milton's poetry. Lines that otherwise might lack color and freshness become truly descriptive and memorable.

In Milton's use of these geographical matters there are discernible three stages. In the first we can observe him under the spell of the classics and the Bible. The youthful poems contain little that reveals what sixteenth-century and early seventeenth-century geographers had discovered. There is, then, a middle period when one becomes increasingly aware that Milton is adding extensively to his knowledge, first by reading in the new geographies, then by travel, and finally by serving in a government capacity where inevitably he learned much about foreign countries. In other words he was slowly undergoing his own personal renaissance. Such authors as Purchas and Fuller and Sandys were gradually replacing the authorities which had been accepted for centuries. The particular books he chose bore some relation to the conditions of the 1650-1660 decade; they were either first issued during those ten years or were translated or had new and important editions. This is true, for example, of books by Fuller and Giles Fletcher, by Diodorus and Heylyn and Olaus Magnus. Their use constitutes Milton's own version of anti-Aristotelianism. Though he advised Mela's *De Chorographia* for the schools, he used Davity's *Les Estats du Monde* in tutoring his nephews. His blindness played its part; there is noticeable after 1652 some tendency to depend on digests.

In the third stage of his development Milton is to be found using the new materials he had assimilated in the earlier period. It is true, however, that what he ultimately did bring over into *Paradise Lost* and the later poems was not necessarily "new." It might be the classics or the Bible seemingly made new by a sixteenth-seventeenth century redaction. On the other hand, enough of the truly new appears to convince us that Milton, as a recent scholar put it, was "picking up knowledge wherever it might be found." And he used that gained knowledge with supreme effectiveness. A single geographic term of a notably specific kind will serve to highlight a whole passage. The technique is comparable with one he learned in his History of Russia: the technique of transposing a telling expression and making it vivify an account of similar circumstances. Almost nobody nowadays holds to the old belief that Milton handles his geographic terms loosely. In fact, research progressively shows the accuracy of his allusions. Together with this accuracy—a quality of even greater importance to poetry—goes an essential *appropriateness*. There are remarkably few instances where the reference does not fit the context.

While it can be maintained that Milton underwent the three stages mentioned above, we should not expect to find any clear-cut divisions between those stages. The early attitude carries over into the second period, and that in turn to the third. His final approach may be classified only as eclecticism. Proserpina and the fair field of Enna come alive again. And the absurd superstitions he so deplored in *A Brief History* find room in *Paradise Lost*. This is as it should be. By 1660 Milton felt there was little material in the heavens above or on the earth beneath that did not constitute the potential stuff of poetry. If it were not so, his great epic would lack many of its qualities of greatness.

The plan of the present volume is briefly as follows. Since commentators have been inclined to mention various writers of travels without serious attempt to determine the relative importance of their influence on Milton, this study aims to supply that lack. At the same time, it aims to estimate in each case the extent and nature of that influence as a whole. It attempts, furthermore, to show the divers ways Milton has used in his poetry the fascinating new information provided by these travel-books.

In the course of the investigations here undertaken it has been found that one travel writer had far and away the most extensive influence. For reasons which will appear, Peter Heylyn held a place in Milton's opinion much higher than any other. The first two chapters of the present book are therefore devoted to an analysis of Heylyn's determining role in connection with the two most important geographic passages in all of Milton, one in *Paradise Lost*, the other in *Paradise Regained*. The third chapter is concerned with the position which Russia held in the poet's mind. Russia was the only foreign country to which he devoted a special treatise. Written in the middle period, his *Brief History of Moscovia* makes it possible to discern differences in Milton's poetry in the nature of the early and late allusions to travel materials. His little History of Russia thus becomes a convenient steppingstone, a middle ground between the sort of general reference he was apt to use in the minor poems and the more specific kind found in his epic. The fourth chapter considers how the poet, even with his obviously increasing knowledge of geography, continued to use the old classical and Biblical geographic materials for their poetic worth. In Chapter v the attempt is made to determine to what extent such travelers as Sandys, Fuller, and Purchas (besides Heylyn) furnished him with information and inspiration. In the final chapter it is shown how Milton skillfully combines the new geographic matter with the old to give his poetry depth and significance.

CHAPTER I

MILTON'S POETIC ADAPTATION
OF GEOGRAPHY

THERE are many passages in Milton's works behind which the reader feels the presence of some writer of exploration and discovery. It may be that such a writer has contributed to the poet a fact or group of facts, he may have contributed an idea, or it may be only an approach or attitude. In time Milton learned which of the many authors to go to for which purpose. Some of them appeared to him most valuable for the information which they afforded; others, for a kind of philosophical outlook, which often involved history. It is natural, in trying to determine the character of these various influences, to go first to those lines of his poetry which contain the greatest amount of geographic material. The study of such lines reveals most clearly the reaction of Milton's mind to travel literature. We can observe in them how he adapted the material and altered it to suit his poetic purposes.

Among all the passages there are two which stand out prominently. The first of these occurs in the Eleventh Book of *Paradise Lost*.[1] It will be recalled that Michael there leads Adam to the highest point in Paradise to show him the future world.[2] In the course of what he has to say, the archangel mentions an unusual number of distant places, all the way from "*Cambalu*, seat of *Cathaian Can*" to "*Mexico* the seat of *Motezume*." Throughout the passage Milton keeps two objectives in mind: one is to impress Adam with the results of his sin by showing him developed

---

[1] L. 370ff.
[2] Some critics have construed the passage too largely as a consolation, basing their judgment presumably on God's injunction to Michael, "dismiss them not disconsolate" (l. 113). But it should be remembered that the angel warns Adam: "good with bad expect to hear" (ll. 358-359).

9

evil; the other, and far more important one, is to stress with
every reader the perversion he and his fellows have made
of God's purpose, the wonder of supernal Grace forever off-
setting Man's sinfulness. Here, then, as usual, the poet and
the protestant are working in harmony. The former is
actively aware of the body and dignity conveyed to his verse
by majestic proper names. As Milton's eyesight got dimmer,
we may assume his hearing grew keener. We know he
reveled in euphonious sounds; and when the amanuensis
read off some particularly mouth-filling word, we can be
sure Milton not infrequently asked that the pleasure-giving
name be repeated. In some few cases doubtless the result in
poetry is tour de force. But usually not. In the passage under
discussion there is no element which does not in some way
contribute to the thought. Masson[3] found "a certain order"
in the lines. It is less an order than a common denominator.
All the regions mentioned serve but to emphasize the
futility and evanescence of human glory. Moreover, not
once is the poet unaware of the poetic effectiveness of pure
sound (he will deliberately change the order of words to
effect that sound); not once does he forget that the names
chosen must contribute, not merely to Adam's sense of guilt,
but to the reader's sense of continuing guilt. Clearly the best
way for him to convey that sense would be through conjur-
ing scenes of earthly splendor. For his "fit audience" such
scenes would carry the connotations of defeat and decay
necessary for the meaning of his passage.

Much has been written lately of Milton's historical knowledge, "so incomparably richer than that of all his poetical
contemporaries put together." And it may be well to see first
what that knowledge consists of through a close analysis
of the lines in question since they are characteristic of the

[3] *Poetical Works* (1894), III, 536. Note also that in the fourth draft of
his tragedy on the fall of man, as given in the Trinity Mss., Milton has an
angel sent to pass before man's eyes "a masque of all the evils of this life
and world."

poet's whole approach. If Milton had not been blind at the time, we should be justified, with such an overwhelming array of proper names, in assuming that he had his finger on some map. Under the circumstances it is perhaps safer to look for some geographic book with which we are reasonably certain he was familiar and which one of his devoted amanuenses might have been reading to him in those dark days following 1652.

Of all such possible books there is one which Milton appears to have relied on most both for his facts and for his point of view. Sufficient evidence[4] exists that he used Peter Heylyn's *Cosmographie* for various passages in his poetry. It is a work which surveys the whole world in brief, a work which, besides including a vast amount of information, has a philosophical approach that would naturally appeal to Milton. The *Cosmographie* was a popular and compendious volume, "contayning the Chorographie and Historie of the whole World, and all the Principall Kingdomes, Provinces, Seas, and Isles, Thereof," published first in 1652 with a second edition in 1657, and then reissued in 1660, 1665, 1666, and 1670.[5] The work is in four books, the first two covering Europe, the third Asia, the fourth being divided into two parts, of which the first describes Africa and the second "containing the Chorography and History of America." A single map precedes each large section, four in all. The volume is provided with elaborate indices, and would be just the sort of book which the blind Milton, no longer able to browse for himself, would direct his assistants to buy. And having bought, he would be apt to use such a work in the passage alluded to above, where he chooses

4 See, for example, Verity's *Paradise Lost*, 1910, p. 460.
5 Heylyn had published an earlier geographical work, called *Microcosmos*, in 1621, which was based on his Oxford lectures and which in turn formed the basis for *Cosmographie*. It may be taken as another example of Milton's broadmindedness that he was willing to accept Heylyn as an authority in matters of geography when he disagreed with him about so many of the fundamental issues in life.

to mention what Heylyn calls "the Principall Kingdomes" all over Asia, Africa, and America.

The detailed analysis which follows will, it is hoped, provide ample proof of the nature and extent of Heylyn's influence on this portion of Milton's epic. Readers will recall that the first region Milton has Michael refer to is,

> *Cambalu,* seat of *Cathaian Can*
> And *Samarchand* by *Oxus, Temirs* Throne (ll. 388-389).

It is possible to identify these allusions, as Milton editors have done, by reference to a number of travel books. But Heylyn[6] alone has these two brief passages:[7]

Principal Cities of the whole at this present time under the notion of *Cathay,* are 1. *Cambalu* . . . *Cambalu,* that is to say, the Seat or City of the *Cham,* in the same sence as the chief City of *China* had the name of *Pequin,* signifying in that Language the Court or *City of the King.*

Marachanda, antient, and of fame, but placed by *Ptolomy,* (why I know not) amongst the Cities of *Bactria*: differing herein from the common and received opinion of other Authors, by whom this City is affirmed to be on the North-side of *Oxus.* . . . It was afterwards called *Samarchand,* the Seat Royall of *Tamerlane.*[8]

Considerable learned ink has been spilled on Milton's two lines. In light of Heylyn the only explanation called for is that, for metrical reasons, the poet chose the well-known original short form of Tamburlaine's name, Temir (Timur).

Much also has been written on the poet's distinguishing, in the next line, between Pekin and Cambalu, between China and Cathay:

> To *Paquin* of *Sinaean* Kings (l. 390).

[6] *Cosmographie,* 1670, pp. 850, 854.

[7] All italics as used in passages for the rest of the chapter are to be found in the original.

[8] Scholars have been bothered by Milton's placing Samarchand "by *Oxus*" (cf. Gilbert's *Geographical Dictionary,* p. 253). That difficulty would seem to be resolved by this passage from Heylyn.

Verity[9] inclines to think that Milton believed in the distinction, and he refers to the misconception prevailing generally until the poet's day. It seems more likely that Milton knew the identity, but for poetic purposes, for wider associational range, he chose to differentiate. Heylyn's evidence on the point is apposite. In one passage[10] he implies his faith in the difference when he says that circumstances "may afford some reason why some Writers easily misguided by such probabilities" might consider Cathay and China "to be one and the same." But, though he chooses in the end to take no side, he adduces, in the course of his argument, four good reasons for thinking the two cities are identical, "which last two evidences coming from the pen of one who had lived many years in *China* . . . must needs be thought to carry some great credit, and authority."[11] In the same section as above[12] Heylyn refers often to "Paquin." And in that section too he frequently alludes to China and the Chinese under the old name of "Sinae"; thus,[13]

It was called antiently *Sinae*, or *Sinarum Regio*, by which name it is still called at the present by our modern *Latinists*; and from whence that of *China* seems to be derived.

It will be recalled that Milton's scene now shifts to India:

To *Agra* and *Lahor* of great *Mogul* (l. 391).

In his own section on India, Heylyn[14] had written under "Pengab":

Places of most importance in it, 1. *Lahor* . . . honoured for a while with the ordinary Residence of the *Great Mogul*, till on

---

[9] *Op.cit.*, p. 596.

[10] *Op.cit.*, 1670, pp. 871-874. In 1657 ed., pp. 873-874.

[11] Gilbert gives additional and pertinent information. See "Milton's China," MLN, XXVI (1911), 199-200. See also his *Geog. Dict.*, pp. 77-78.

[12] The whole section on "China" is only eleven pages long. Verity is wrong in implying (p. 625) that Heylyn regularly spells the name "Pequin." It is "Paquin" at III, 208, 209 (twice) in the 1652 edition. That is the form also in *Microcosmos* (1636), pp. 682, 683.

[13] *Cosmographie*, 1652, III, 206.   [14] *Op.cit.*, 1652, III, 220.

the burning of his Palace, spoken of before, he removed his Court to *Caximir*, from thence to *Fatipore*, and at last to *Agra*.

And two pages later Heylyn[15] wrote:

The Realm of *Agra*. . . . So called from *Agra* the chief City of it, and the Seat Royall, of late times, of the Great *Monguls* [sic].

From the above cities we are rapidly taken by Milton,

> Down to the golden *Chersonese* (l. 392).

This region also Heylyn[16] had referred to in that same section on "India":

The Countrey of greater length than breadth, stretcheth it self South-wards into the Sea many hundred miles, in form of a *Peninsula* or *Demy-Iland*, called antiently *Aurea Chersonesus*, or the Golden Chersonese.[17]

Milton now transports us westward again,

> where
> The *Persian* in *Ecbatan* sate, or since
> In *Hispahan* (ll. 392-394).

Under "Persia" Heylyn[18] has,

Cities of most note in it [Major Media], 1. *Ecbatana*.[19] . . . In former times the ordinary residence of the Monarchs of the *Medes* and *Persians*.

And the second city mentioned by Heylyn, as Ecbatana was the first, is,

Tauris, situate in or neer the place of *Ecbatana*, out of whose rubbish it was built.

This probably accounts for a matter that puzzled one critic,[20]

---

[15] *Op.cit.*, III, 222.   [16] *Op.cit.*, III, 241.

[17] Heylyn again has "the *Golden Chersonese*" at III, 254. D. J. Gordon (RES, July, 1942, pp. 318-319) relates Milton's other mention, "the golden *Chersoness*" (*P.R.*, Bk. IV, l. 74), partly for orthographic reasons, to *Orlando Furioso*. But cf. Heylyn's *Microcosmos*, p. 413, "Chersonesse."

[18] *Op.cit.*, III, 159.

[19] This is the exact spelling used by Milton in his other reference, *Paradise Regained*, III, 286.

[20] See A. H. Gilbert, *A Geographical Dictionary of Milton*, p. 109. On pp. 286-287 Professor Gilbert shows how common the confusion was.

who wrote: "Milton incorrectly identifies it [Ecbatana]
with the modern Tabriz (Tauris)." On the second Persian
city mentioned by the poet Heylyn[21] wrote,

Hispaan, commonly called *Spahan,* or *Spawhawn,* raised out of
the ruins of *Hecatompyle,*[22] and as that was, the Regal City for
these parts.[23]

From Russia and Turkey,[24] next referred to, we are taken
south to,

> Th' Empire of *Negus* to his utmost Port
> *Ercoco* and the less Maritine Kings
> *Mombaza,* and *Quiloa,* and *Melind,*
> And *Sofala* thought *Ophir* (ll. 397-400).

It has been argued[25] with some convincingness that this
passage is largely taken from Ortelius. This particular critic
quotes, for instance, a passage offering an explanation of
"Negus": "The same whom we in *Europe* call *Presbyter
John,* or *Priest John,* the Moores call Anticlibassi, themselves,
that is, the Abyssines or Ethiopians, Acegue and Neguz,
that is Emperour and King." On the other hand, Heylyn[26]
has: "The *Abassines* themselves are of this opinion, and
therefore in the stile of the *Neguz* (so they call their

---

[21] *Op.cit.,* III, 172. [22] Cf. p. 31, note 20 *infra.*
[23] On the change of royal residence from Ecbatan to Hispahan, Gilbert
(*op.cit.,* pp. 146-147) quotes a very pertinent passage by Cartwright from
Purchas' *Pilgrimes.*
[24]   or where the *Russian Ksar*
In *Mosco,* or the Sultan in *Bizance,*
Turchestan-born (ll. 394-396).
There is no use in more than pausing on these lines since the facts contained were common knowledge. There is no use even in pointing out
that "Mosco" is Heylyn's spelling (cf. II, 154) because that was one of the
regular ways to spell the word. The rather unusual spelling *Ksar* (see
note p. 64 *infra*) may be due to Milton's desire, seen elsewhere (cf. pp.
18 and 19), to sound the word as near to the original (Caesar) as possible. As for "*Turchestan*-born," Heylyn (*op.cit.,* III, 196) broaches the
theory only to question it; under "Turchestan" he writes: "That their
whole body settled here, and from hence made their conquest of *Persia,*
as some very industrious men are of opinion, I by no means grant." It is
exceptional for Milton to go against Heylyn's authority.
[25] See G. W. Whiting's *Milton's Literary Milieu,* pp. 119-120.
[26] *Op.cit.,* 1670, p. 981.

Emperour) he is termed King of *Goiamy*." And this passage
is on the next page to the one on Mount Amara which
Milton almost certainly used in Book IV, 28off.[27] The chief
argument in favor of Ortelius consists in the spelling of
"Ercoco." The above-mentioned scholar is quite right in
saying that this spelling, which is given on Ortelius' map
of Abyssinia, is somewhat unusual in the maps. Heylyn's
spelling is regularly "Erocco."[28] Mombaza, Quiloa, and
Melinde are also in Ortelius. But here Heylyn has important
evidence to present: "Melinde," "Mombaza," and "Quiloa"
all appear on the same page and in large letters so that the
reader's eye would naturally catch them.[29] On the next page
(75) Heylyn says under "Sofala" (also in large letters):
"This Country for its abundance of *Gold* and *Ivory*, is by
some thought to be that land of *Ophir*, to which *Solomon*
sent."[30]

Milton now transfers us to the western coast of Africa:

> to the Realme
> Of *Congo*, and *Angola* fardest South (ll. 400-401).

Heylyn[31] has "MANICONGO. . . . So called from *Congo* or

[27] Cf. pp. 69-70 *infra*.

[28] See *op.cit.*, III, 151; IV, 59, 66. In the voyagers, however, Milton's
spelling is not infrequently met. Cf. Purchas' *Pilgrimes*, I, 308, 315; VII,
212, 393. And Leo Africanus uses that spelling. See *History and Description*, I, 27, 30. Leo's general map of Africa also has "Ercoco." Davity has
"Ercocco." See *The Estates, Empires, and Principallities of the World*,
trans. by E. Grimstone, 1615, p. 1079.

[29] *Op.cit.*, IV, 74. A feature that should certainly not be overlooked is,
as Verity says (*op.cit.*, p. 626), that all three places were well-known
centers of trade, particularly for the Portuguese. It seems gratuitous, however, in the light of Heylyn's passage, for him to go on to mention Camões,
who refers to some of the same names in his *Lusiads*. All these names
appear prominently in Heylyn's map of Africa preceding Book IV. Verity
is wrong, moreover, in implying that Milton had the *city* of Quiloa in
mind, "on a small island"; it was rather the country as shown on Heylyn's
map. He is wrong, too, in his next note (p. 627), when he says that Milton "is alluding to the town of Sofala." The passage in Heylyn which
Milton was presumably following (*Cosmographie*, IV, 75) makes it quite
clear that it was the country.

[30] "Sofala" does not appear on Ortelius' map of Ethiopia.

[31] *Op.cit.*, IV, 78-79.

Manicongo, the principal of those many Kingdoms which are united in this Name." And under that, the first place to be printed in large letters, "Angola": "The principal of those [provinces] that be, are 1. ANGOLA."[32] The word is not merely set off in bold print but heads a new paragraph.

The poet then works his way up along the coast into the north of Africa:

> Or thence from *Niger* Flood[33] to *Atlas* Mount
> The Kingdoms of *Almansor, Fez* and *Sus,*
> *Marocco* and *Algiers,* and *Tremisen* (ll. 402-404).

For some reason Heylyn chooses to play up "Mount Atlas," printing the name[34] in letters equal in size to the broad divisions of the continent, larger indeed than "Egypt" and equal to "Aethiopia Superior." He begins his account: "In our way from *Barbarie* to *Libya Interior,* we must pass over *Mount Atlas,* a ridge of hills, of exceeding great heighth, and of no small length. So high that the top or *Summit* of it is above the clouds, at least so high that the eye of man is not able to discern the top of it." Heylyn[35] furthermore identifies "Almansor," whom Milton refers to: "*Rabut* or *Rubut,* built by *Mansor,* or *Almansor,* a King of *Morocco.*" And eight lines below he speaks of the town "Salla" as having been "beautified by King *Almansor* (who is here interred)." The name is repeated a second time on that

[32] Both Congo and Angola appear prominently on Heylyn's map of "Africa" preceding Book IV. "Angola" is also mentioned in connection with trade in one of the "Skinner Letters." See *Works,* XIII, 461. For everything except the poetry, the edition referred to will be the Columbia, 18 vol., New York, 1931-1938. The Oxford edition is used for the poetry.

[33] "The riv. Niger" is naturally a prominent feature of Heylyn's map. But that means little since Niger and its approximate location were well known to Milton. Under "Terra Nigritarum" Heylyn speaks (*op.cit.,* IV, 54), of the river's being "of as long course, and the same wondrous nature, as the River *Nilus.*"

[34] Bk. IV, 48. Before his blindness Milton might have read at length about Atlas in Leo's *Description of Africa.* Note reference to Leo in the *Commonplace Book, Works,* XVIII, 139.

[35] Bk. IV, 39. Thompson gives this reference. See "Milton's Knowledge of Geography," SP, XVI, 161, note 19.

same page. It is noticeable that the unusual spelling is exactly Milton's.

The evidence that Milton followed Heylyn in mention of the five kingdoms of Almansor is far less convincing. All five are to be found in the *Cosmographie*, but two of them usually in different form. "Fesse," in large print, occurs on pages 35, 38, and 39. On page 40 Heylyn writes: "The whole called *Fesse*, from *Fez*, an *Arabick* word, signifying *Gold*."[36] And on his map of "Africa" the town is spelled "Fez," the kingdom "Feze." Leo, on the other hand, whom Gilbert[37] quotes, regularly spells "Fez." As for the second name in the list, on page 36 Heylyn has "the Province of sus or susa, so called from the River *Sus*."[38] "Morocco," again in large letters, appears on pages 35, 36, 37, 42, 43, and 44, with the second letter regularly "o." It is true that Heylyn has "Marochi" in his map of "Africa," or "Marocho" in his general map at the beginning of Book I. But Leo, whom Gilbert[39] quotes in this connection too, usually has "Maroco." It can, of course, be argued that Milton deliberately chose a form as close as possible to the original Arabic (Marakish or Marrākesh).[40] We should not need to lay this much emphasis on spelling if there were not abundant evidence in the passage under discussion that Milton took great care with that feature. Similar problems arise with the last two names. Algiers was, of course, well known in trade and in piracy; but to the seventeenth century that particular spelling

[36] This reference given by Verity (*op.cit.*, p. 627). The town appears as "Fez" in Heylyn on page 43 (three times).

[37] *Geographical Dictionary*, p. 122. Furthermore, Gilbert (*op.cit.*, p. 123) quotes a passage from Leo referred to in Milton's *Commonplace Book*, showing the poet's acquaintance with the *Description of Africa*. This is the passage alluded to in *Works*, XVIII, 139.

[38] Verity is wrong (*op.cit.*, p. 627) in identifying it with modern Tunis. Leo describes the region of "Sus," *op.cit.*, II, 248ff.

[39] *Op.cit.*, p. 184.

[40] That tendency in him may be seen in such uses as "Motezume" (see p. 19 *infra*) and "ammiral" (see Verity, *op.cit.*, pp. 695-696). He spells "Marocco" also in *Animadversions* (see *Works*, III, pt. I, 169).

was quite unusual. One comes across Argier, Argiers, Alger, and Algier. When Milton referred to it in *Eikonoklastes*,[41] he used "Argiers." Leo's regular form is "Alger" in the text, and in his map it appears "Algier." In Heylyn it is "Algiers."[42] However, he equates "Tremesen, or Algiers," whereas Milton keeps them distinct. Once more, Heylyn's spelling is closer than Leo's,[43] who usually has "Telensin," though he will give "Tremizen" in the margin. In his map Heylyn distinguishes between the two, using exactly Milton's spelling "Tremisen"[44] but having "Alger" for the second. However inconclusive may be the spelling test in the above two lines, the fact remains that Heylyn has for "Almansor" exactly the same form as the poet; that he mentions in large letters all five places referred to, and those on three consecutive pages, 34-36.

After Europe Milton shifts to the western world:

> in Spirit perhaps he also saw
> Rich *Mexico* the seat of *Motezume* (ll. 406-407).

The richness of Mexico was, from early times, proverbial. Heylyn's spelling of the Indian emperor's name is "Motecuma."[45] Milton's omission of the "n" has been commented on by scholars. It may be another case, like "Marocco," of the poet's preferring an earlier form since, as Verity[46] tells us, the Aztec name was "Moteuczoma," corrupted by the Spaniards into "Montezuma."[47]

Milton glances finally at South America:

> And *Cusco* in *Peru*, the richer seat
> Of *Atabalipa* (ll. 408-409).

[41] See *Works*, v, 282.   [42] *Op.cit.*, iv, 34.   [43] *Op.cit.*, ii, 659.

[44] Ortelius also has this spelling in his map of Barbary. See 1612 edition of *Theatrum*, map following p. 117.

[45] *Op.cit.*, iv, 134 (three times). The name is apt to appear without the "n" in the English voyagers. Cf. Hakluyt and Purchas.

[46] *Op.cit.*, p. 628.

[47] Peter Martyr spells "Muteczuma."

Under "Peru" Heylyn[48] has "Cusco," the only city printed in large letters under the country of the same name. About it he says that it was "once the seat-royal of the *Ingas* or *Peruvian* Kings." As for the comparative wealth of Mexico and Peru, Heylyn[49] has under "Nova Hispania": "The Country is inferiour to *Peru* in the plenty and purity of *Gold* and *Silver.*" It is noticeable that he does not spell the Indian emperor's name like Milton. He has a variety of spellings, "Atabilaba, or Athnalpa," "Athualpa, *or* Atubaliba," and "Atabaliba."[50] The last is fairly regular in the voyagers, being the one used by Purchas in his *Pilgrimage.* In the *Pilgrimes,* on the other hand, he has "Atabalipa."[51] Since "Atahualpa" is closer to the Indian, of which "Atabalipa" is the Spanish corruption, we have here a case in reverse, where Milton has preferred the newer spelling.

From Peru we move to Guiana:

> and yet unspoil'd
> *Guiana,* whose great Citie *Geryons* Sons
> Call *El Dorado* (ll. 409-411).

On the "yet unspoil'd *Guiana*" Heylyn[52] has, at the con-

---

[48] *Op.cit.,* IV, 153.

[49] *Op.cit.,* IV, 132. Under "Cusco" Heylyn (*op.cit.,* IV, 153) speaks of "*Mines* of such Riches, that the Kings part out of them amounteth yearly to above 40000 *Pezoes,* which is about 130000 l. of our *English* money." Much of the account of Peru is taken up with its fabulous wealth. See especially the beginning (IV, 149) and, still more strikingly, the end (IV, 157).

[50] *Op.cit.,* IV, 153, 156, 171.

[51] This is the spelling used by Ortelius also. See *Theatrum* (1612 ed.), p. 9. Purchas resorts to other forms in *Pilgrimes;* "Atahualpa" and "Atabaliba" appear and, in one instance, "Atahualpa" and "Atabalipa" occur on a single page. In Hakluyt the form is almost regularly "Atabalipa." Perhaps it is significant that that is also the spelling in Ralegh's *Discovery of the Large, Rich, and Beautiful Empire of Guiana.* Whiting has shown the probable considerable dependence of Milton on Ralegh's *History of the World.* See *Milton's Literary Milieu,* esp. pp. 39-62.

[52] *Op.cit.,* IV, 153. Gilbert (*op.cit.,* p. 135) quotes a passage from Ralegh which may well explain the "yet unspoil'd *Guiana.*" The following passage in Heylyn's description of Manoa (*op.cit.,* IV, 171) may also be pertinent: "For though the *Spaniards* and the *English* have severally sought, and that with incredible diligence to find out this City, yet none of them have hitherto had the fortune to fall upon it."

clusion of that short account (less than a page) of "Cusco": "Beyond the *Andes* lie some Countries much famed for wealth: the discovery whereof hath often been attempted by the *Spaniards,* sometimes with loss, not seldom with some hopes of a better fortune, but hitherto without success." Under "Guiana" itself he[53] speaks of "the great and famous City *Manoa,* which the *Spaniards* call *El Dorado.*" Milton's "*Geryons* Sons" have long been identified as the "Spaniards."[54]

Let us try to visualize what may have happened. In November of 1656 Milton[55] is writing to his friend Peter Heimbach, thanking him for having found the price of a certain atlas in which Milton was interested. That price—130 florins—seemed to him overwhelming: "Since to me at least, on account of my blindness, painted maps can hardly be of use, vainly surveying as I do with blind eyes the actual globe of the earth, I am afraid that the bigger the price at which I should buy that book the greater would seem to me my grief over my deprivation." Clearly what was passing through the poet's mind in those days was that a less expensive atlas without color would serve as well or better the purpose of a man whose sight was completely gone. In the next year appeared the second edition of Heylyn's *Cosmographie.* It was a work perfectly suited to his use. In the first place it was reasonably authoritative and it was,

---

[53] *Op.cit.,* iv, 170. Gilbert (pp. 111-112) again quotes appositely from Ralegh's narrative.

[54] Professor Osgood (*The Classical Mythology of Milton's English Poems,* p. 37) associates Geryon, a mythical Spanish king, with gold, citing Diodorus, who says Geryon was killed by Heracles because of his gold. Osgood quotes a passage from *Faerie Queene* (v, x, 9, 1-4) where Spenser speaks of "the sonne of Geryon."

Some significance is to be attached to Milton's having introduced a classical name and story among all these "modern" names. It is significant also of course that Guiana came to be thought of through Ralegh as partly an English project.

[55] *Works,* xii, 83-85.

for the time, compendious. It covered the whole known world and its descriptions were correspondingly brief. If Milton wished to know more of strange countries or if he wished to refresh his memory about countries less strange, he could hardly have selected better. From this volume (or from the first edition) one of the devoted amanuenses could have read in comparatively brief time the passages which might have inspired Milton's poetic imagination.

When, therefore, the artistic exigencies of the now famous lines in Book xi required that Milton should swiftly survey the world, a book like Heylyn's would furnish just the information he needed. A lesser poet would have depended on his general knowledge, however vague. Milton did not work that way; what he wrote he wanted right, and though that "right" might in some particulars have been wrong, it was the seventeenth century and not he that was in error. Clearly what he wished the passage partly to convey was a sense of great glory which was destined to decay because of the perversion of God's purpose for which man alone was responsible. Thus the word "destind" which happens to precede the "Walls of *Cambalu*" is intended to apply to the whole passage in question. As one reads the accounts of the various kingdoms and empires in Heylyn, one is impressed by the uniformity with which the author insists on the splendor and magnificence of the regions described. But one notices too that Heylyn usually calls attention to the decay. Thus of Samarchand he writes[56] that it is "farr short of that magnificence which once it held." Further it is noticeable that Milton emphasizes the conquered Montezuma and not the conqueror Cortes, Atabalipa, and not Pizarro. And the whole tragedy and fiasco of Ralegh are visible through the concluding lines. The poet took full advantage of all the overtones associated with the once glorious kingdoms he mentions. And it can be argued

[56] *Op.cit.*, iii, 195.

that, for a Puritan, he appears to revel in the magnificence of those connotations.

As the amanuensis read the notable passages aloud, Milton reveled too in the pure sound of names, though that aspect was naturally secondary with him. Most of those names were already familiar to him from his earlier readings in travel literature and through the importance of some of them in trade, and especially familiar perhaps because of his years in government capacity, dictating letters to foreign governments about commercial infringements against his countrymen.

In all this Heylyn may have acted like a catalytic agent, bringing together Milton's knowledge of many books. No memory, not even Milton's, could have recaptured so many names in their proper connections and correct forms. A work like the *Cosmographie* was necessary, and probably it was being read to him in or near the time when he was actually composing the twenty-five lines. It would have been unlike Milton, however, to restrict himself to one book. There is evidence enough to indicate that for Africa he supplemented with Leo's authoritative *History and Description*, and for America he had in mind as well Ralegh's *Discovery of the Large, Rich, and Beautiful Empire of Guiana*. There is a good possibility that he also used Purchas.

If his dependence on Heylyn is as extensive here as it appears to be, we need not even raise the question of Milton's poetic originality. Shakespeare could alter a single word in North's *Plutarch* and make of prose transcendent poetry. Milton in the same way insisted that whatever is borrowed must be bettered by the borrower if it is to be called his at all. "Golden Chersonese" may appear in the original; but the magnificent cadence of "down to the golden *Chersonese*" is Milton's and Milton's alone.

CHAPTER II

FURTHER CHARACTERISTIC USES OF
GEOGRAPHIC MATERIAL

IT HAS been customary to associate the passage discussed in the previous chapter with one in *Paradise Regained*.[1] In the latter, one can observe equally well how Milton resorted to Heylyn, how once more he took over from him proper names, and how he may even have been influenced by some of his underlying ideas regarding the geographic matters. The passage in question shows Satan conducting Christ to a mountain top and revealing to him "all the kingdoms of the world, and the glory of them." The similarities, both circumstantial and poetic, are obvious. Satan like Michael seeks to impress Christ ("our second *Adam*") with the magnificence of worldly possessions and power. Milton clearly wishes in both passages to warn his reader against the temptation of a life of luxury and the wrong kind of power, and the results of such a corruptive life. But there are differences, too, in situation and approach:

> Not higher that Hill nor wider looking round,
> Whereon for different cause the Tempter set
> Our second *Adam* in the Wilderness,
> To shew him all Earths Kingdomes and thir Glory
> (*P.L.*, Bk. xi, ll. 381-384).[2]

Adam needed to be shown the awful consequences of his act; Satan, falling into his usual error of judging other people by himself, misconstrues Christ's character by assuming He can be appealed to by some of the very things Michael proved to be wrong. There is, however, a broad

[1] Bk. iii, ll. 267-321.
[2] For a good recent study of the various problems underlying the Temptation, see E. M. Pope's *Paradise Regained: The Tradition and the Poem*, Baltimore, 1947. Miss Pope shows the seventeenth-century preconceptions and some of the surprising changes Milton elected to make. Cf. especially pp. 12 and 112-114.

basis of comparison between the two passages in question; Milton's purpose in both is to stress the evanescence of human glory and the downright evil contained in ease and extravagance. The Puritan is to be discerned almost as much in one as the other. Furthermore, there is no appreciable difference in the sheer pleasure the poet takes in splendid proper nouns. If one is looking for poetic progress, perhaps one can find it in the way the later passage is better integrated into the whole story. It has been called more historical; but it is more historical only in the sense that Milton relates the events more closely to the experience of Christ. The skillful way in which the poet keeps bringing us back to the Bible will become clear in the later detailed analysis.

As in practically everything that Milton wrote, there is in the passage a considerable amount of what most people knew. Any educated person knew about Assyria, the Caspian Sea, the Indus and Euphrates Rivers; he had read about Babylon and Cyrus and the Parthians. But Milton was never satisfied to leave matters there. He was always bringing his material into focus by mention of some vivifying detail which was not so well known. No poet better knew the effect of such phrases as "inaccessible the *Arabian* drouth," "of length within her wall several days journey," and "the drink of none but Kings." These are the additions which regularly keep Milton's verse from becoming commonplace, the additions construed by naïve critics as a show of his learning.

Being learned, he could not write naturally without showing it. In the present passage his purpose was to convey the general background, which everybody knew, but to bring that background into relief by a number of matters by no means so familiar. His mind was richly stored with historical and geographical information; but he pointed and sharpened that information by resort to the best recent authorities. And here once more is where the amanuenses come in.

Many explanations have been offered for how the blind poet could possibly have written a passage so full of exact detail. A good case has been made[3] for his having used Pliny and the maps, notably two maps of Ortelius and several of Ptolemy. But Heylyn played his important part too. The combination of historical with geographic which Milton needed for his passage would be just what he would find in the *Cosmographie*. It will be remembered that Satan reveals the great empires of the world in succession: Assyrian, Babylonian, Persian, Macedonian, Parthian. The general outline of conquest and rule would, of course, be known to many. Broad divisions such as Sogdiana, Arachosia, Hyrcania, and Susiana appeared on most maps; and mention of those must therefore be largely discounted as affording any help in determining specific sources. But Heylyn rendered an extraordinary amount of detailed information besides. It could be that Milton asked his amanuenses to describe for him what the maps contained. But again it appears more credible that he should request those same amanuenses to read to him passages from Pliny and from Heylyn. Such passages would sink into his poetic consciousness and come forth, perhaps in those magnificent bursts of inspiration which the early biographers have described for us.

At any rate Heylyn has an unusual number of details, even of the exceptional kind, which Milton introduces in these lines. Two matters have been specially commented on by scholars,[4] who have remarked that "Candaor" (l. 316) and "*Balsara's* hav'n" do not exactly belong, being more "modern" than most of the others. It is noteworthy that

---

[3] See G. W. Whiting's *Milton's Literary Milieu*, pp. 91-92, 123-124.

[4] See, for instance, Gilbert, *op.cit.*, pp. 46 and 72. Cf. also Todd's (*Poetical Works*, v, 187) quotation from Sir W. Jones, as well as Jerram's note (*Paradise Regained*, p. 135), and Hughes' (*Paradise Regained*, p. 502).

Heylyn[5] speaks of *"Balsora,*[6] the Port Town to *Babylon,"*
and emphasizes its prominence by referring to its "great
wealth and trading." Further, two lines below he says it is
"supposed to be the City of *Teredon."* Milton alludes to
Teredon in line 292. Still further, a little above on the same
page Heylyn prominently mentions *"Ctesiphon,* on the
River *Tigris,* not far from *Seleucia,* by whose fall it rose
. . . , beautified and walled by *Pacorus,* a *Parthian* King;
and by him made the Seat-Royall of the *Persian* Kingdome."
Milton, it will be noticed, refers to Ctesiphon twice (ll. 292,
300) in association with the Parthians. And in line 291 he
refers to Seleucia. Again, "Adiabene," which Milton introduces in the line just before *"Balsara's* hav'n," is described
by Heylyn on the next page (131).[7] In the case of "Candaor,"
the same inferences may be drawn. Heylyn[8] speaks of
"Paropamisus" which is "now by some called *Dache,* by
others *Candahor."* On the same page he displays "Arachosia" prominently (mentioned by the poet in same line).
And on that same page he refers to *"Choaspes* the chief
River of *Media"* (cf. *P.R.,* Bk. III, l. 288).

There are other ways in which the Milton passage recalls
Heylyn's work. The River Araxes (l. 271), for instance, is
mentioned by the cosmographer five times on a single page
(III, 164).[9] In his following lines the poet skillfully weaves
geography and history:

---

[5] *Op.cit.,* III, 130.

[6] All italics here and in quotations for the rest of the chapter appear in
the original.

[7] This mention of Adiabene may help to explain another of Milton's
lines (274):

> And inaccessible the *Arabian* drouth.

Under the general heading "Assyria," Heylyn (*op.cit.,* III, 131-132)
writes: *"Adiabene,* bordering on *Mesopotamia,* so called; . . . , or inaccessible, because fenced with such unfordable Rivers, *Tigris,* and *Euphrates,*
that there was no easie comming to it." Adiabene is shown on the maps
as being bounded on the west by Tigris. Across the Euphrates lies Arabia
Deserta.

[8] *Op.cit.,* III, 169-170. "Candahor" is repeated twice on the same page
(170).

[9] On p. 143 (Bk. III) Araxes is mentioned first of the "Chief Rivers of
this Countrey." And it is again alluded to on p. 196.

Here *Ninevee*, of length within her wall
Several days journey, built by *Ninus* old (ll. 275-276).

Pliny, whom Whiting[10] cites, makes no mention of the several days' journey. Heylyn[11] speaks of,

Nineve, by the *Greeks* and *Latines* called *Ninus*;[12] first built by *Nimrod*, and called *Ninive* with relation unto *Ninus*, his sonne or Nephew. . . . A City so enlarged by some of the succeeding Kings, that it came at last to be bigger than *Babylon*, in compass 480 furlongs, or 60. miles; and therefore said in the Book of *Jonah*, to be a City of three dayes journey, in circuit, as indeed it was; accompting 20 miles for a dayes journey.

Gilbert[13] aptly quotes Diodorus who, like Milton, gives Ninus as the builder. On the other hand, Gilbert feels it necessary to quote "Jonah" separately, a passage which in this connection may have been brought to the poet's mind by Heylyn.

The Bible appears also in Milton's next reference when he describes Nineveh as the,

seat of *Salmanassar*, whose success
Israel in long captivity still mourns (ll. 278-279).

It has been usual for commentators to cite II Kings 17:1-6, where the account is given of Israel's Ten Tribes' being led into captivity by Shalmaneser. Here too, however, is a place where Heylyn skillfully combines geography with history. In his short account of Assyria, within ten lines of his mention of Adiabene and on the same page where he describes Nineveh, Heylyn[14] has:

[10] *Op.cit.*, p. 92. See *Nat. Hist.*, II, 27.

[11] *Op.cit.*, III, 132. A few pages later (136) Heylyn writes: "*Ninus* . . . removed the Imperiall Seat to *Ninive*, by him much beautified and inlarged."

[12] It was the Greek theory that Nineveh was founded by Ninus. See Strabo's *Geography* (London, 1917), I, 319.

[13] *Op.cit.*, pp. 209-210.

[14] *Op.cit.*, III, 132. In two other passages where he refers to the monarch he spells his name exactly as Milton does. In one (III, 163) he speaks of a town in Susiana inhabited largely by Jews, "supposed to be the descendants of those whom *Salmanassar* transplanted out of the Kingdom of

One of them [Assyrian cities] to which the *Ten Tribes* were transplanted by *Salmanasser*, 2 *Kings* 17.6 and 18.11.

In the lines that follow, the Bible continues to play its part, though it may have done so from suggestions offered by the *Cosmographie*:

> There *Babylon* the wonder of all tongues,
> As antient, but rebuilt by him who twice
> *Judah* and all thy Father *David's* house
> Led captive, and *Jerusalem* laid waste,
> Till *Cyrus* set them free (ll. 280-284).

Here is an allusion to two more historical events, Nebuchadnezzar's twice leading the Jews into captivity and their being set free by the Persian Cyrus. These are naturally well-known happenings; but the way in which Heylyn introduces them bears considerable resemblance to Milton's version. He speaks[15] first of "*Babylon* . . . the antientest City in the World . . . in the place destinated to the raising of the Tower of *Babel* . . . much increased both in bulk and beauty by *Nabuchadnezzar*, who therefore arrogated to himself the whole glory of it, saying in his pride, *is not this the great* Babel *that I have builded? Dan.* 4.30. A City of great fame and state, accompted one of the worlds nine wonders. . . . How it fell into the hands of *Cyrus*,[16] we learn out of

---

Israel." A third mention appears in the account of Palestine itself (III, 105): "When *Salmanassar* had subdued and captivated the ten Tribes of *Israel*, he sent new Colonies of his own to plant this Countrey." Heylyn alludes to him also at III, 60, 61, and 159. In the 1657 edition, which of course Milton could have used, the spelling is regularly "Salmanassar" (see pp. 697, 761, 788, 819).

The spelling appears to have been somewhat unusual in Milton's day, though it is close to the Vulgate. Giles Fletcher Sr. wrote a tract called *A Discourse Concerning the Tartars*, part of whose title is "captivated by Salmanaser" (see *Russia at the Close of the Sixteenth Century*, Hak. Soc. Publs., vol. XX, 1856, p. cxxvi). Fuller (*Pisgah-Sight*, 1650, p. 55) has "Shalmaneser" and "Salmaneser" (p. 190).

In this connection Professor Charles Fritsch of the Princeton Theological Seminary kindly verified some details for me.

[15] *Op.cit.*, III, 129.

[16] Ezra 1:7 speaks of Cyrus' having returned rich vessels stolen from Jerusalem by Nebuchadnezzar.

Xenophons Cyri-paideia." All this occurs on the page preceding the mention of Ctesiphon, Balsora, and Teredon.

Milton next refers to Cyrus' capital:

Persepolis
His City there thou seest (ll. 284-285).

Heylyn[17] gives a detailed description of the splendors of Persepolis. But this fact is of no great significance because the city and its reputation were so well known.[18]

The poet had shown his familiarity with Ecbatana when he wrote in *Paradise Lost* (Bk. xi, l. 393) that "The *Persian* in *Ecbatan* sate." Here he alludes to the city again:

Ecbatana her structure vast there shews (l. 286).

Heylyn[19] gives the city a prominent position in his narrative:

Cities of most note in it [Media], 1. *Ecbatana*, of as great antiquity as *Babylon*. . . . For beauty and magnificence little inferiour to *Babylon* or *Ninive*, before described. In compass 180 or 200 Furlongs, which make about 24 *Italian* miles. The walls thereof affirmed in the book of *Judith* to be 70. *Cubits* high, 50. *Cubits* broad, and the Towers upon the Gates 100 *Cubits* higher.

He goes on then to speak of the seven walls, "each of them higher than the other." And finally of the "Royall Palace being about a mile in compass," which "was built with all the cost and cunning that a stately mansion did require." Two lines below, Milton has mentioned Susa (l. 288). On the same page with the passage quoted above Heylyn has

[17] *Op.cit.*, iii, 164. He cites the passage from Diodorus which Gilbert quotes in this connection (*op.cit.*, pp. 230-231). Actually Heylyn's account is in part a paraphrase of Diodorus.

[18] Heylyn's description of Persepolis occurs on the same page where he mentions the River Araxes five times. On the decay of the city Hakluyt (iii, 154) has a pertinent passage: "In the way of his [Geoffrey Ducket's] travel he passed through Persepolis, sometime the roiall seate of the Emperors of Persia, but now altogether ruined and defaced, whereof remaine to be seene at this day two gates onely."

[19] *Op.cit.*, iii, 159. This is on the same page with Atropatia (cf. *P.R.*, Bk. iii, l. 319), which he gives in large letters.

joined the two cities, speaking of Ecbatana as formerly "the ordinary residence of the Monarchs of the *Medes* and *Persians* in the heats of the summer, as *Susa* (the chief City of *Susiana*) in the cold of winter."

In his long list Milton includes also,

> *Hecatompylos* her hunderd gates (l. 287).

Heylyn[20] has,

> *Hecatompyle*, the Royall City, so called from the number of an hundred Gates in the walls thereof.

The following lines have called forth much comment:[21]

> There *Susa* by *Choaspes*, amber stream,
> The drink of none but Kings (ll. 288-289).

Heylyn[22] puts Susa on the Eulaeus River, usually identified with the Choaspes:[23]

Susa . . . honoured with the residence of the *Persian* Monarchs in winter, as *Ecbatana* in summer. Situate on the River *Eulaeus*.

And on the previous page (162) he had written:

Eulaeus, the chief River of *Susiana* . . . : a River of so pure a stream, that the great *Persian* Kings would drink of no other water.

That the Persian kings would drink of no water but Choaspes was a well-known legend.[24] Pliny and Herodotus, among others, mention the fact. But commentators have gone to too much pains to explain why Milton should have made the water exclusively the drink of monarchs. He found that so absolute a statement fitted best the purpose served by these particular lines.

[20] *Op.cit.*, III, 172. Two lines below, he mentions "Hispaan," which Milton may have used in *Paradise Lost*, Bk. XI, l. 394. See pp. 14-15 *supra*.
[21] See, for instance, Todd's long note in his *Poetical Works*, V, 177-179.
[22] *Op.cit.*, III, 163.
[23] Cf. Pliny, *op.cit.*, V, 484: "The kings of Parthia drink no water but that of the Choaspes or of the Eulaeus." Elsewhere (II, 79) he says, "the river Eulaeus . . . flows round the citadel of Susa."
[24] See *Paradise Regained* (ed. E. H. Blakeney), p. 140.

Milton now proceeds with his history:

> of later fame
> Built by *Emathian*, or by *Parthian* hands,
> The great *Seleucia* (ll. 289-291).

Here the poet is close to Pliny,[25] who speaks of "Ecbatana, the capital of Media," which "was built by king Seleucus, at a distance from Great Seleucia of seven hundred and fifty miles." Heylyn, however, seems still to be in his mind. Continuing the passage quoted above[26] on Babylon and Nebuchadnezzar, the *Cosmographie*[27] describes how the city passed from Persian into Macedonian hands:

After this taking of it by the *Macedonians*,[28] the glories and magnificence hereof began to decline. . . . That wondrous change occasioned partly by the injury of time, partly by the neglect of the *Macedonians*, who removed the Seat Royal of their Empire more towards *Greece*: but principally by *Seleucus Nicanor* [sic], who offended with the *Babylonians*, built the City of *Seleucia*.

Heylyn[29] then proceeds to describe this Seleucia, "the second City of note in all this Countrey. . . . Nor did this new City rob the old onely of its power and greatness." He had stressed this greatness also on the previous page when he referred to "*Seleucia*, successour unto *Babylon* in repute and greatness."[30]

The next city alluded to by Milton is Nisibis. This also is given some prominence by Heylyn,[31] who speaks of it as "a City of great note in those elder times." Of the three places that follow, Artaxata, Teredon, Tesiphon, the first is prominently mentioned by Heylyn[32] and called "of most esteem

---

[25] *Op.cit.*, II, 28.   [26] See p. 29 *supra*.   [27] Bk. III, 129.

[28] Milton used *Emathian* for *Macedonian*, as he did in Sonnet VIII, l. 10.

[29] It appears probable that Milton was familiar with this passage since Ctesiphon, Balsora, and Teredon appear within a page of it.

[30] Milton had mentioned "Great *Seleucia*" in *P.L.*, Bk. IV, l. 212. Whiting (*op.cit.*, pp. 49-50) is inclined to trace this reference to Ralegh's History.

[31] *Op.cit.*, III, 134 (wrongly printed 136).

[32] *Op.cit.*, III, 144.

in those times, and the Seat-royall of the Kings of *Armenia* from its first foundation"; the second, Teredon, has already been referred to[33] as appearing in the *Cosmographie*[34] and being identified with Balsora; and the third is, of course, the same as Ctesiphon, which was described by Heylyn on the same page with Teredon.[35] Milton speaks of these cities as being "of later fame" and of being built "by *Parthian* hands." Heylyn describes how Ctesiphon superseded Seleucia, as that had done Babylon, how it was built by Vardanes and "afterwards beautified and walled by *Pacorus*, a *Parthian* King."

Milton now visualizes the conquest of great Arsaces:

> All these the *Parthian*, now some Ages past,
> By great *Arsaces* led, who founded first
> That Empire, under his dominion holds
> From the luxurious Kings of *Antioch* won (ll. 294-297).

The passage contains well-known historical facts. And Heylyn gives them corresponding emphasis. At the top of his list of Parthian kings he gives[36] "*Arsaces*, the founder of the *Parthian* family." And six pages earlier[37] he had written: "During whose reign [Seleucus Callinicus, one of "the *Syrian* Kings"], *Arsaces* a noble *Parthian*, provoked by some indignities, slew the Governour, and took the estate upon himself, persuading all the rest of the Provinces to do the like: and thrived so well in his design, that he not onely gained the Kingdome of *Parthia*, but united to it all the Provinces lying on the East of *Euphrates*." The importance of these events is indicated by the fact that Heylyn describes them again on page 178, in addition to referring to Arsaces' conquests on pages 173 and 176.

[33] See p. 27 *supra*. [34] Bk. III, 130.
[35] See p. 27 *supra*.
[36] *Op.cit.*, III, 179. Cf. also (1670) p. 824: "*Arsaces*, the founder of the *Arsacidan* race of the Kings of *Persia*."
[37] *Op.cit.*, III, 173. This passage is within a page of "Hispaan" and "Hecatompyle." See p. 31 and note 20 *supra*.

Heylyn does not ordinarily resort to the title, "Kings of *Antioch*," as Milton calls them. Usually with him it is "Kings of Syria"; thus in the passage about Arsaces' victories referred to above, he[38] says the Persians gained nothing when Arsaces freed them from Greek yoke, "these *Parthian* Princes lording it with as high an insolencie, as ever . . . the Kings of *Syria*, did before." In his earlier account[39] of Syria and Antioch he referred to the city as being "the Royall seat for many Ages of the Kings of *Syria*" and to its being "adorned in former times with many sumptuous Palaces, and magnificent Temples, answerable to the reputation of so great a City." (Cf. "luxurious Kings," l. 297 of the poem).

Milton goes on to describe the preparations for battle:

> for now the *Parthian* King
> In *Ctesiphon* hath gather'd all his Host
> Against the *Scythian*, whose incursions wild·
> Have wasted *Sogdiana* (ll. 299-302).

Ctesiphon was a logical place for him to put the assembling of troops since it was of the Parthians' own building and used by them, according to Heylyn, as the "Seat-Royall."[40] R. C. Browne[41] conjectures that by "Scythian" Milton meant "Turk." But Heylyn[42] under "Sogdiana," which he spells in large letters, speaks of a city "on the borders of the *Scythians*; against whose invasions or irruptions it was said to be built." And just below he alludes to a city built by Cyrus, "to fortifie his borders against the *Scythians*." Milton's mention of Parthian methods of fighting,

> Steel Bows, and Shafts their arms
> Of equal dread in flight, or in pursuit;
> All Horsemen, in which fight they most excel (ll. 305-307),

[38] *Op.cit.*, III, 178.

[39] *Op.cit.*, III, 60. The "King of *Antioch*" in the same paragraph refers to a later period. Many of the kings had "Antiochus" in their title.

[40] See p. 27 *supra*. Strabo (*Geography*, VII, 219) says that the Parthian kings made it their winter residence to spare the Seleucians from having the "soldiery quartered amongst them."

[41] *English Poems by Milton*, II, 311.   [42] *Op.cit.*, III, 194.

should perhaps go unmentioned as being so familiar a circumstance. Heylyn[43] does, however, in his short section on "Parthia" lay considerable stress on what "Good horsemen" the Parthians were, on their being "such lovers of the warres, that they accompted no man happy after his decease but who died in battell." And he concludes: "But their greatest fame consisted in the handling of their *Bow and Arrows*, esteemed the best *Archers* in the world, and not undeservedly; having the Art of shooting backwards, and making their Retreat or flight more terrible, than their charge or onset."[44]

After mention of the cities through most of his lines, Milton concludes by enumerating several of the provinces. The first he gives is "Arachosia" (l. 316). It has already been seen[45] how it and "Candaor" (Candahor), next mentioned, are given by Heylyn on the same page, the first of them in large letters. "Margiana," Milton's next name, is also printed by Heylyn[46] in large letters.

> And *Margiana* to the *Hyrcanian* cliffs
> Of *Caucasus*, and dark *Iberian* dales (ll. 317-318).

"Hyrcania" appears prominently in the *Cosmographie*, heading the section just before Margiana. But the conjecture, advanced by Gilbert[47] and others, that by "Hyrcanian" the poet meant "Caspian" is certainly right because the Caucasus

---

[43] *Op.cit.*, III, 171. It has been customary here for commentators to quote Phineas Fletcher, *Purple Island*, canto xi, st. 48, which refers to the Tartars.

[44] On the following lines M. Y. Hughes (*Paradise Regained*, p. 501 note) quotes an apposite passage from Montaigne, based on Ammianus Marcellinus.

Professor Hanford discusses Milton's picture in "Milton and the Art of War" (SP, XVIII, 1921, 260-262), concluding that he has added to Parthian arms "the complexity and splendor of Persian, Roman, Carthaginian and Macedonian warfare, making it stand symbolically for the glamor of arms in general." The formations mentioned, Hanford says, are mostly to be found in Aelian.

[45] See p. 27 *supra*.

[46] *Op.cit.*, III, 174.   [47] *Op.cit.*, pp. 150-151.

mountains are not near Hyrcania. Thus Heylyn[48] says: "HYRCANIA is bounded . . . on the North, with the *Hyrcanian* or *Caspian* Sea." As for the "dark *Iberian* dales" Heylyn,[49] under the heading "Iberia," has, "The Countrey for the greatest part, is covered with Mountains, woods, and thickets."

In his concluding lines Milton writes:

> From *Atropatia* and the neighbouring plains
> Of *Adiabene, Media,* and the South
> Of *Susiana* to *Balsara*'s hav'n (ll. 319-321).

Heylyn[50] has "Atropatia" in large letters on the same page where he describes Ecbatana.[51] As one province of Assyria he[52] mentions "Adiabene." It was long ago noted[53] that Strabo refers to the country's plains. Just below Atropatia on page 159 Heylyn gives *"Major Media, or Media"* (large letters) "where one may see plenty of green Meadows." Moreover, the *Cosmographie* has "Susiana" in large letters on page 162.[54] And finally, as has already been shown,[55] Milton may have taken *"Balsara*'s hav'n" from a passage in Heylyn, which contains also Ctesiphon and Teredon.[56]

It is dangerous to reason that Milton was following any one book just from the fact that an historical geography

[48] *Op.cit.,* III, 173. Cf. also Pliny, II, 30: "Beyond the river Sideris the Caspian begins to take the name of the 'Hyrcanian' Sea." Heylyn may have reminded Milton of the famous Virgilian lines (*Aeneid,* IV, 366-367) since he quotes Virgil's description in this very passage. It has been usual for commentators (cf. Gilbert and Hughes) to cite Virgil in this connection.

[49] *Op.cit.,* III, 147. Gilbert (*op.cit.,* p. 151) quotes a significant passage from Purchas' *Pilgrimes,* which speaks of a province in Georgia as being covered with a "thicke and palpable darknesse."

[50] *Op.cit.,* III, 159. Pliny uses the longer form "Atropatene." Cf. Holland's Pliny (1601), I, 122.

[51] Cf. p. 30 and note 19 *supra.*

[52] *Op.cit.,* III, 131. Pliny also has Adiabene. Cf. Holland, I, 122.

[53] Cf., for example, Todd's note, *op.cit.,* V, 187.

[54] Pliny appears not to have included this province.

[55] Cf. p. 27 *supra.*

[56] Whiting (*Milton's Literary Milieu,* p. 49) quotes Ralegh's History to prove how people of that time identified Teredon and Balsora. The same identification was made by Ortelius. See Gilbert, *op.cit.,* p. 46.

describing the same regions should happen to group together many of the same names. But some further passages in Heylyn are at least suggestive. In two lines (p. 162), for instance, he mentions Susiana, Parthia, Arachosia, Hyrcania, and Margiana. Later (p. 173), also in two lines, he refers to "*Hyrcanian* or *Caspian* Sea," Margiana, Atropatia, and Media.

It has not been the purpose of the foregoing study to establish that Milton used Heylyn by any means exclusively. It is likely that the maps played their important part. And certainly Pliny must have been somewhat in the poet's mind. There are cases where Pliny's spelling squares better with Milton's than does Heylyn's. On the other hand, there are an extraordinary number of names in the *Cosmographie* which appear in Milton and which appear under circumstances that indicate that the poet may well be indebted to the cosmographer. Virtually all of the passages cited and quoted from Heylyn occur within a comparatively few pages, from pages 129 to 195. To an unusual extent— especially for the seventeenth century—the spelling is identical in the two authors. And this is all the more remarkable when we consider that many of the names were long and little known. Quotations from classical authors, Herodotus, Pliny, Diodorus, Tacitus, which have been cited by editors in illustration of Milton, are repeated by Heylyn; he thus becomes once more a kind of catalytic agent, bringing together much material the poet found he could use. Finally, Heylyn interweaves history with geography in a way that strongly suggests Milton's practice.

The observation has been made above that Milton appears to have taken rather more care to integrate the whole passage with the rest of the story than he did in *Paradise Lost*. In composing the lines he clearly had two objectives. He wished first to impress his reader with the worthlessness

of earthly glory. And, second, he hoped somehow to inter-
relate the events with the experience of Christ Himself. Thus
Nineveh becomes the seat of Salmanassar, that Salmanassar
whose success, the Devil says, *your* people, the Israelites, still
mourn in their captivity. And Babylon was rebuilt by the
Nebuchadnezzar, "who twice *Judah* and all thy Father
David's house led captive, and *Jerusalem* laid waste." Further, the events are specifically related to the time of Christ.
Parthia was nearly at the height of its power; only fifty
years before Christ's birth, the great Roman general Crassus
had been overwhelmed and slain by Parthian forces. There
are at present, says Satan, two great ruling empires, the
Roman and Parthian, and he advises Christ to get control
first over the latter, "found able by invasion to annoy thy
country" in spite of anything the Roman can do. This
implication of Parthian superiority is found in Heylyn also.
In the passage on Ctesiphon[57] he says the city was "many
times besieged and assaulted by the *Roman* Emperors; but
most commonly without success." And again[58] he maintains
that the Parthian princes "kept the *Romans* harder to it,
than all the Kings and States in the world besides." The
long description of Parthian arms serves not merely the
poetic purpose of relieving the monotony of a series of
names; it serves also to impress Christ with the nation's vast
strength.

The element that gives the passage its supreme unity is
the element of *decay*, implied or stated. There is always
something unsound beneath the splendor and apparent
strength. Milton could count on the readers' normal associations of effeteness and decadence with such cities as Nineveh
and Babylon and Persepolis.[59] And the very fact that many
of those readers might be unfamiliar with Ecbatana and

[57] *Cosmographie*, III, 130. See p. 27 *supra.*
[58] *Op.cit.*, III, 178.   [59] Cf. pp. 29-30, note 18 *supra.*

Hecatompylos would make them assume that the "structure vast" and "hunderd gates" had passed away. Sometimes the poet chooses to be explicit as in "the luxurious Kings of *Antioch*." Even the Parthians, with all their display of force, won by treacherous methods and "overcame by flight." It is worth mentioning that Heylyn, preacher that he was, almost invariably calls attention to the deplorable decay associated with these vanished civilizations. On Babylon, for instance, he writes,[60] that "the glories and magnificence hereof began to decline," and that it was "reduced to desolation in the dayes of *Pliny*." And on the next page he makes a special point about another of the cities mentioned: "*Ctesiphon*, . . . not far from *Seleucia*, by whose fall it rose; occasioning the decay thereof, as that did of *Babylon*." Of the royal palace in Ecbatana he said[61] that, being "neglected by the Kings of the *Parthian* race, it became a ruin." About Antioch itself, whose kings Milton referred to as "luxurious," Heylyn[62] had written: "The glories of this famous City so declining after this last *Tragedy* . . . that it is grown the sepulchre of what once it was, and lieth buried in its own sad ruines; hardly preserving the repute of a sorry village. Such is the instability of all worldly glories." Here was doctrine that would deeply impress the Puritan.

Poetically the passage is just as characteristic. The fact that Milton dares to put eleven proper nouns (or the adjectives based on them) in only thirty-four words, practically one in three,[63] shows that he has lost none of his fondness for pure sound. But he has saved himself from list-making by individualizing the people and places named. He thus succeeds in raising the picture into relief. Nineveh is "of that first golden Monarchy the seat," and Choaspes flows with its "amber stream." Here lies the explanation of the much

[60] *Op.cit.*, III, 129.
[62] *Op.cit.*, III, 60.
[61] *Op.cit.*, III, 159.
[63] Ll. 316-321.

discussed "drink of none but Kings" (l. 289). Practically all the sources say merely that the kings would drink of no other water except the Choaspes (or Eulaeus). The effect of Milton's change is to individualize the river still further.[64]

The other way in which these lines are typical is, of course, in the emphasis they lay on details of warfare. Professor Hanford[65] showed how deep that interest went. One has only to read *A Brief History of Moscovia* to see how Milton's mind naturally grasped military affairs. He was outstandingly well informed on the subject, and he found here a proper place to use that information. Starting with Parthian methods he has, before he finishes, included Persian, Macedonian, Roman, and Carthaginian. And all the display contributes perfectly to his climax when Christ says:

> Much ostentation vain of fleshly arm,
> And fragile arms, much instrument of war
> Long in preparing, soon to nothing brought,
> Before mine eyes thou hast set (ll. 387-390).

This is Milton repeating in poetry what he had so eloquently urged years before in his *Second Defence of the People of England*:[66]

And unless that liberty which is of such a kind as arms can neither procure nor take away, which alone is the fruit of piety, of justice, of temperance, and unadulterated virtue, shall have taken deep root in your minds and hearts, there will not long be wanting one who will snatch from you by treachery what you have acquired by arms.

Thus Milton has used two of his interests, the military and the splendor of outworn civilizations, so to speak, negatively. As poet he almost reveled in the complicated ma-

---

[64] This same individualization may be seen in the way he used his sources in *A Brief History of Moscovia*. See R. R. Cawley, *Milton's Literary Craftsmanship*, esp. pp. 16-17 and 29.

[65] SP, XVIII (1921), 232-266.

[66] *Prose Works* (Bohn Edition), London, 1848-1853, I, 295.

neuvers of rhombs and wedges, half moons, and wings, in the glory that was Babylon and the grandeur that was Parthia. As Puritan he could imply the unsoundness which lay beneath it all. And both contributed materially to the artistic perfection which is *Paradise Regained*.

CHAPTER III

MILTON AND RUSSIA

THOUGH Milton implied that it was somewhat by accident[1] that he chose to describe Russia, the fact remains that Russia is the single foreign country about which he has left us an extended description. *A Brief History of Moscovia* makes clear, as much from what he omitted of Hakluyt and Purchas as from those matters he included, what especially interested Milton in the country. To him it stood for cold, for tyranny, for drunkenness and ignorance. In other ways it appealed to him because "no man [was] forc'd to Religion,"[2] and no man was condemned to live with a wife who was unworthy;[3] in fact, it was a country where the man sent his fiancée a whip in token of her absolute subjection. Further, if monarchs there proved immoral or deceptive, the people did not hesitate to rise and kill them. It was undoubtedly partly through his official position that Milton came to interest himself in and to know so much about Russia. He saw at first hand the profound effect on trade relations which Charles' execution wrought;[4] the Czar naturally did not fancy the precedent.[5] Of course,

---

[1] Cf. Preface to *A Brief History of Moscovia, Works*, x, 327. "I began with Muscovy, as being the most northern Region of Europe reputed civil."

[2] *Works*, x, 343.

[3] Was it only chance that made Milton put these two ideas together: speaking of Shusky, he wrote that he "never married, of great wisedom reputed" (*Works*, x, 361)?

An entry in his Commonplace Book carries its own significance: "John, son of Basil, duke of Moscow, divorced his wife (the custom of his country permitting him not as king alone but any man to do this as often as he wished)." See *Works*, xviii, 157.

[4] See letter to Russia for which Milton was responsible. *Works*, xiii, 301. The letter, addressed to the Duke of Russia, speaks of "how Ancient the Friendship, and how vast the Trade has bin for a long train of years between the *English* Nation and the People of your Empire."

[5] Sir William Foster (TLS, April 6, 1933, p. 248) maintains that the lack of bookishness about Milton's geographical references is due in part to his intimate acquaintance with the growth of English trade.

the state department was not the only channel through which the poet received his information. *A Brief History* is a patchwork, albeit an artistic one, of materials carefully collected from the pages of Hakluyt and Purchas. Besides, in his Preface Milton had specifically alluded to Paolo Giovio's *Moschovia* and had particularly commended Giles Fletcher,[6] "whose Relations being judicious and exact are best red entirely by themselves." The suave Baron von Herberstein had issued his *Rerum Moscoviticarum Commentarii*[7] in 1549 though Englishmen had not yet taken sufficient interest in the book to have it translated. Eden in *The History of Travayle*[8] had a section called "A briefe description of Moscovia, after the late writers, as Sebastian Munster, and Jacobus Gastaldus." *Sir Thomas Smithes Voiage and Entertainment in Rushia* appeared in 1605. And Gerrit de Veer's account of Barents' three voyages to the northeast had been englished in 1609,[9] and had clearly done much to set the impression of those regions.[10]

There was another reason why Milton and other Englishmen should have taken so lively an interest in Russia. Trade with her had been opened up, so to speak, fortuitously since the early explorers had stumbled on her while seeking the

[6] *Works*, x, 378. *Of the Russe Common Wealth* was originally printed in 1591. This was the edition the Muscovy Company succeeded in getting suppressed for fear it might give offence to the Russians. The work was issued in 1643 (?) as the *History of Russia*.

[7] See *Notes Upon Russia*, Hak. Soc., 2 vol. (vols. 10 and 12), London, 1851-1852.

[8] F. 271ff. (wrongly numbered 274).

[9] See modern edition, *Three Voyages by the North-East*, Hak. Soc., vol. 13, London, 1853. Another "background" book that will prove helpful to the reader is *Early Voyages and Travels to Russia and Persia* (Hak. Soc., vols. 72, 73, London, 1886), which contains the travels of Anthony Jenkinson and other Englishmen and has a long introduction with much useful information. Still another volume is the translation of J. Hamel's work, entitled *England and Russia* (London, 1854).

[10] Heylyn devotes a section to Russia in which he purveys most of the characteristics normally ascribed to the country. See *Cosmographie*, II, 150ff. Cf. also the Elzevir *Russia* (1630).

northeast route to Cathay.[11] When the English found Spanish and Portuguese largely preempting the southern routes
to East India, they naturally turned their attention to the
north. And the expedition of 1553, led by Sir Hugh Willoughby, set forth with the sole purpose of discovering a
northeast passage. Failing there, Chancellor, second in com-
mand, won through to Moscow and began negotiations with
the great Ivan Vasilowich. Willoughby, perishing of cold
in "bleak Arzina's road," Chancellor, Burrough, Jenkinson,
and the rest thus became some of the noblest of English
heroes. How the northeast route was regarded as a pe-
culiarly *English*[12] project may be read in *A Brief History*.
In his very Preface Milton speaks of "the more northern
Parts thereof, first discovered by *English* Voiages." And
throughout the essay the same note is sounded. National
pride is implicit in the way he belittles the Russian "fine
houses"; in the way he makes a grand finale for Chapter IV
by declaring that the Russian-Polish peace was brought about
"partly by the mediation of King James"; in telling how the
Emperor ordered the points of English religion to be read
to his nobility "with much approbation"; and in the obvious
relish with which he tells how the brash Jerome Bowes
refused to be impressed with the Czar's position.[13] There
is some emphasis also on Ivan Vasilowich's suing in vain
for the hand of Lady Mary Hastings and on Dr. John Dee's
having refused a flattering offer from the Emperor. One
last thing which *A Brief History* brings out is Milton's eagerness to learn new facts about foreign countries; certainly
he feels satisfaction in the advantage he has over Paolo

[11] Milton (*Works*, XIII, 504) writes proudly of the English being "the
1st that ever traded with him [the Duke of Muscovy] from these parts by
the Northern sea."

[12] This is shown further by the fact that in his second edition Hakluyt
gave the North first place.

The tradition goes far back; in his *History of Britain* (*Works*, X, 131)
Milton speaks of Arthur's having conquered "all the North East Iles as
far as *Russia*."

[13] Cf. *Works*, X, 375-376.

Giovio and in the information added by late Russians, "who describe the Countreys in their way far otherwise than our common Geographers."[14] It is while speaking of the latter that he mentions the great delight he took in following their discoveries.

To be sure, Milton did not rise so much above his countrymen in allowing a low opinion of the North in general to color his impression of Russia. Russia was, so to speak, discovered by the north and she must therefore share in that region's reputation. Witches, sorcerers, the devil himself hailed from the North; Richard Barckley[15] had referred to "an old saying" that "all evils rise out of the north." And George Abbot[16] had been no more complimentary: "The countrie is colde, the people barbarous, . . . in some part of the yeare there is no night at all." Thus when in his first *Defence*[17] Milton bids his adversary, "go take along with you your plaguy teaching to utmost Siberia and the Arctic Ocean"; or when, describing the terrible effects of the fall, he says perpetual spring might else have smiled on all the earth,[18]

> except to those
> Beyond the Polar Circles,

he is not being more condescending than the rest.[19] In short, northern peoples were backward, ignorant, and barbarous. It is significant that of Giles Fletcher's book readers chose to believe only the unfavorable part, though Elizabeth's ambassador had gone to some pains to show the obverse, to describe the country's fruitfulness, and its delightfulness at certain times of the year:[20]

[14] See Preface.
[15] *Felicitie of Man* (1598), p. 327.
[16] *A Briefe Description of the Whole Worlde*, 1599, fol. D1.
[17] Cf. *Works*, VII, 285.
[18] *P.L.*, Bk. x, ll. 680-681.
[19] For the North's reputation with other writers of Milton's time see R. R. Cawley, *Voyagers and Elizabethan Drama*, pp. 256-257.
[20] *Russia at the Close of the Sixteenth Century*, Hak. Soc., 1856, p. 6.

In the sommer time you shall see such a new hew and face of a countrie, the woods (for the most part which are all of fir and birch) so fresh and so sweet, the pastures and medowes so greene and well growen (and that upon the sudden), such varietie of flowres, such noyse of birdes (specially of nightingales, that seeme to be more lowde and of a more variable note then in other countries), that a man shall not lightly travell in a more pleasant countrie.

Further he praised the common soldier for his ability to endure incredible hardships. The Muscovy authorities, however, knew well what they were doing when they succeeded in getting the edition suppressed since they realized Englishmen would remember only the derogatory parts. And when thirty-four years later Purchas[21] chose to reprint Fletcher, he wisely "mollified the biting or more bitter stile, which the Author useth of the Russian Government; that I might doe good at home, without harme abroad."[22]

When we come to consider the reflection of Milton's knowledge of Russia in his poetry, we find the problem quite different from the one in the previous chapters. There we discovered sufficient reason to believe that the blind poet was having read out to him from the pages of Heylyn passages which proved useful in the poetry he was at just that time composing. Here, on the contrary, the poet is for the most part recalling sections which he had himself been able to read a good ten years before. In his usual thoroughgoing manner he had, while preparing for his *History of Moscovia*, traversed Hakluyt and Purchas with great care and had selected just those parts which he considered good geography. The very nature of his task made him master of the material. In any such process it would be quite possible that some parts discarded would come to find their place

---

[21] See *Pilgrimes*, XII, 499 margin.
[22] On the other hand, Milton's contemporary, Heylyn, continued the severe indictment.

later in his poetry; the stone which the builder rejected might indeed become the head of the corner.

It is not unreasonable to look in *Paradise Lost*, therefore, for evidences of the reading Milton was doing, probably sometime in the forties,[23] in Russian affairs. He has forthrightly left us his list of authorities, at the end of *A Brief History*; most of them, it is noticeable, are eyewitnesses because he invariably preferred their evidence to others', such accounts as "the Journall of Sir Hugh Willowby," the "Discourse of Richard Chancelor" and "Another of Clement Adams taken from the mouth of Chancelor." Generally speaking, the information as given in his poetry is not so fresh in his mind. But there is evidence that here too he was having the amanuensis pull down some dusty volume from the shelf. Usually, however, the feeling one gets is that the poet is reproducing only what made considerable impression on him years before. For instance, still insisting on the awesome effects of man's first disobedience, he writes:

> Now from the North
> Of *Norumbega*, and the *Samoed* shoar
> Bursting thir brazen Dungeon, armd with ice
> And snow and haile and stormie gust and flaw,
> *Boreas* and *Caecias* and *Argestes* loud.... (Bk. x, ll. 695-699)

And we recall at once that one of *A Brief History's* five chapters was called "Of Samoedia, Siberia, and other Countries north-east subject to the Muscovites"; further that Milton had read not merely Purchas, on which this particular chapter was based, but the accounts as well from Hakluyt of Willoughby's harrowing experience in neighboring regions, the incredible stories of Giles Fletcher, who recorded that water thrown up froze before it had a chance to reach ground. He had read too, doubtless, Gerrit de Veer's detailed narrative of Barents, in which every other sentence, it

[23] See, for instance, G. B. Parks, "The Occasion of Milton's *Moscovia*," SP, XL (1943), 399-404.

seems, reflects the withering cold which the Hollanders
endured.

The very fact that Milton should have devoted so much
space in *A Brief History of Moscovia* to lands lying *east* of
Russia (he has two chapters) shows first how he regarded
the country as but a way-station to Cathay, and second how
he was by nature interested in those east-lying and little-
known regions. His dwelling upon such features as the
great din of bells, the men armed in iron from hand to foot,
the lake in which grew rubies and sapphires, the fabled Wall
prove how willingly he allowed himself to be drawn in
delight after the travelers. He has perhaps forgotten his
own caveat in the Preface that he would eschew "absurd
Superstitions, Ceremonies, quaint Habits." The Russians
whom Milton is following are by now of course at the very
borders of Cathay, with the great Wall stretching from
Boghar to the North Sea four months' journey, "with continual Towers a flight-shot distant from each other, and
Beacons on every Tower." There is nothing to justify Verity's assumption[24] from this account that Milton consistently
distinguished Cathay from China. In fact, as Gilbert[25]
points out, Purchas, whose book we know Milton was
thoroughly acquainted with, has a long discussion of the
possible identity of the two. In all probability, therefore,
when in *Paradise Lost*[26] the poet has Michael distinguish
between "the destind Walls of *Cambalu*" and "*Paquin* of
Sinaean Kings," we have merely another instance where
Milton has chosen to serve his poetic purpose.

Another place frequently associated by Englishmen with
Russia was the Caspian Sea. This too was perhaps inevitable
since there was a close connection through trade. The
English had felt out the route over Archangel, up the Dvina,
then through Vologda to the Volga, and by way of that

[24] *Paradise Lost*, p. 596. Cf. p. 13 *supra*.
[25] *Op.cit.*, p. 77.
[26] Bk. XI, ll. 387-390.

river to Astrakhan and the Caspian into Persia. One of the great pioneering heroes, Anthony Jenkinson, had taken this route. And while on the Caspian he had weathered terrible storms. At one time, with cable broken and anchor lost, all on board looked for "present death." Later "there arose another great storme, at the Northeast, and we lay a trie, being driven far into the sea, and had much ado to keepe our barke from sinking, the billowe was so great."[27] Three years later[28] he had no better luck, "the storme and sea being growen very sore." This particular storm battered his ship for seven days. We know from *A Brief History* that Milton followed Jenkinson's adventures carefully, that he consulted the very pages in Hakluyt which told of these incidents. Is it any wonder that the poet, wishing to drama-tize the threatened struggle between Satan and Death, should have done so in these terms:

> As when two black Clouds
> With Heav'ns Artillery fraught, come rattling on
> Over the *Caspian*, then stand front to front
> Hov'ring a space, till Winds the signal blow
> To joyn thir dark Encounter in mid air (Bk. ii, ll. 714-718).[29]

In *A Brief History*[30] he had taken straight over from Hak-luyt, by his own admission, the notable passage about Jen-kinson's having encountered "between the said Rost Islands and Lofoot" a strange whirlpool. Also by his admission he had lifted the detail from a later voyage of Jenkinson of the Englishman's having come to Moscow just at the time when the Emperor was about to be married to a Circassian lady.[31] Between these two—sixty-one pages after the first and

---

[27] Hakluyt, *op.cit.*, ii, 476-477. [28] *Ibid.*, iii, 19.

[29] Literature before Milton had had, of course, allusions to the Caspian's storminess. Cf. *The Faerie Queene*, ii, vii, 14, 1-5; and Marlowe had visualized the Sea as "ever-raging" (*Works*, 1865, p. 9). Verity is inclined to associate the reference with romances, and instances Fairfax's Tasso. It seems to me far more likely that Milton derived it from the voyagers.

[30] Cf. *Works*, x, 370 with Hakluyt, ii, 415.

[31] Cf. *Works*, x, 372 with Hakluyt, iii, 16.

twenty-eight pages before the second—comes the description of Caspian's storminess.[32] Actually the second account of the storm occurs in the very same narrative with that of the Emperor's impending marriage, within three pages. Here then is probably an instance where Milton felt no call to mention the circumstance in his prose but allowed it later to find a place in *Paradise Lost*.

Another north-lying country often associated with Russia was Lapland. And here the strongest tradition was that of witches. In *A Brief History*[33] Milton chooses to repeat the story of Shusky's having "consulted with Witches of the *Samoeds, Lappians* and *Tartarians*" about the succession, and being warned that "one Michalowich" would succeed. Milton was certainly aware of the tradition.[34] But the fact that such reputable authors as Purchas and Giles Fletcher Sr. vouched for the truth gave it a kind of currency. "For practise of witchcraft and sorcerie," wrote the latter,[35] "they passe all nations in the worlde." In light of this fact, a passage in *Paradise Lost* takes on added meaning. In conveying the horrible impression of Sin's offspring, Milton compares them with the loathsome train of the Night-Hag as she comes swooping through air,

> Lur'd with the smell of infant blood, to dance
> With *Lapland* Witches (Bk. ii, ll. 664-665).[36]

[32] Other passages are still closer. Cf. *Works*, x, 335-336 and Hakluyt, ii, 455 ("They hang up their fish," etc.) where the interval is only twenty-one pages.

[33] See *Works*, x, 361.

[34] For its extensiveness, see R. R. Cawley, *Voyagers and Elizabethan Drama*, pp. 250-252.

[35] Hakluyt, *op.cit.*, iii, 404.

[36] Another way in which voyages *en route* to Russia may have conditioned Milton is in his description of the whale, with which he compares Satan:

> that Sea-beast
> *Leviathan*, which God of all his works
> Created hugest that swim th' Ocean stream:
> Him haply slumbring on the *Norway* foam. . . . (Bk. i, ll. 200-203)

It would seem to be no mere coincidence that the whales Jenkinson noticed, "very monstrous hard by their Ships; whereof some by estimation sixty

On the other side of Russia, Milton picked out for special mention the Obi River.[37] He describes Satan, looking the world over for the creature into which he will enter to deceive the mother of mankind, as follows:

> Sea he had searcht and Land
> From *Eden* over *Pontus*, and the Poole
> *Maeotis*, up beyond the River *Ob*;
> Downward as farr Antartic (Bk. ix, ll. 76-79).

Here clearly Milton is concerned with extremes. The "River *Ob*" is intended for a kind of Ultima Thule. As Obi was known to be a Siberian river and as Siberia stood for everything cold, it was a natural selection for the poet to make. But it was a selection that went counter to some recent discoveries. England had made progress since William Warner[38] wrote, "It is no common Labour to the River Ob to sayle." The very materials which Milton worked through for *A Brief History* had passages which indicated that the river was in no sense a *ne plus ultra*; following Purchas, he

---

foot long; they roard hideously, it being then the time of their engendring" (*Brief History, Works*, x, 371), should have been "about *Zeinam*" off the Norwegian coast. In the Burrough voyage "toward the river of Ob" the mariners saw a "monstrous Whale" beside their ship, which they dared not attack "for feare hee should have overthrowen our shippe." See Hakluyt, *op.cit.*, ii, 336. In all the controversy about what Milton meant exactly by "Leviathan" (see Verity's *Paradise Lost*, p. 710), it is of interest to observe that Heylyn under "Norwey" (*Cosmographie*, ii, 132) calls whales leviathans outright.

In another controversy, over Milton's source for the story of sailors mooring by the whale's side, thinking it an island, I disagree with Professor Thompson (sp, xvi, 169), who believes the poet was more apt to derive the detail from Ariosto. I regard the older ascription, to Olaus Magnus, as the more likely, especially since Milton had had the work called to his attention by a recent translation at just the right time (1658).

[37] Stephen Burrough had brought the river into some prominence with Englishmen. See Hakluyt, *op.cit.*, ii, 322: "Navigation and discoverie toward the river of Ob . . . by Master Steven Burrough." As we have seen, Burrough was one of the outstanding national heroes.

[38] *Albion's England*, Chap. lxvi. Warner was proud of his own father's being one who "did, through the seas of ysie rocks, The Muscovites disclose" (Chalmer's *English Poets*, iii, 634). G. C. Taylor (*Milton's Use of Du Bartas*, Cambridge, Mass., 1934, p. 55) quotes Sylvester's "stately Ob."

speaks[39] in fact of "the River Ob. Beyond which, the *Muscovites* have extended lately their dominion." Indeed, some of the recent associations with Obi were anything but cold. A seasoned English merchant, with many years of experience in those regions, speaks of a "Sea beyond Ob" which "is by the report of the Russes, that are travailers, so warme, that all kinde of Sea fowles live there as well in the Winter as in the Summer."[40] And Milton was so deeply impressed by this unusual circumstance that he made it the finale for the third chapter of *A Brief History*. Here then was a case where he deliberately chose, in poetry, to disregard what appeared to be new information. In general, this was apt to be his practice in passages, such as this, where he was indicating extremes.

Among Russian customs, Englishmen visualized the Muscovites as fighting an almost continuous war with the Tartars. Milton had devoted quite a little space to this rivalry in his *Brief History*.[41] He speaks there of the Tartar Prince Bathy's having subdued the country, of how the second wife of Ivan Vasilowich by strategy freed her country of Tartar yoke, of how "*Juan Vasiliwich* . . . vanquish'd the *Tartars* of *Cazan* and *Astracan*," and of how the Crim Tartar burst into Russia in 1571 and burnt Moscow to the ground. Milton had plenty of authority for this emphasis. Besides Hakluyt he had Giles Fletcher,[42] who maintained that the Tartars invaded about once a year. And Heylyn[43] wrote: "The *Eastern* parts are vexed with the *Tartars*; who like *Esops* dog, will neither dwell there themselves, nor suffer the *Muscovites* to plant Colonies in them."

[39] *Works*, x, 333.

[40] Purchas, *op.cit.*, xiv, 296. There is some evidence that the explorers concerned were using their imagination.

[41] See *Works*, x, 350-353.

[42] *Russia at the Close of the Sixteenth Century*, pp. 85 and 86. Note also Eden's *History of Travayle* (1577), f. 300: "But agaynst the *Tartars*, and especially the *Tartars* of Europe, called the *Precopites*, the *Moscovites* have oftentymes kepte warre with good successe, in revenge of the injuryes done to them by theyr incursions."

[43] *Op.cit.*, ii, 152.

Clearly Milton was perfectly aware of the literary tradition built on history. After all, even Chaucer had sung in the *Squieres Tale* of a Tartar king who had "werreyed Russye." Later Beaumont and Fletcher had made Russo-Tartar warfare an essential part of *The Subject*. More important still are allusions by Spenser and Phineas Fletcher. The former,[44] describing Prince Arthur's fight with Maleger, uses this figure:

> And in his flight the villein turn'd his face
> (As wonts the Tartar by the Caspian lake,
> Whenas the Russian him in fight does chace).

Fletcher[45] proves what a good Spenserian he was, but goes on to add a detail to the master's description; he is describing a titanic struggle between the forces of Good and Evil:

> As when by Russian Volgha's frozen banks
> The false-back Tartars fear with cunning feigne,
> And poasting fast away in flying ranks,
> Oft backward turn, and from their bowes down rain
> Whole storms of darts; so do they flying fight:
> And what by force they lose, they winne by slight;
> Conquerd by standing out, and conquerours by flight.

This element of the Tartars' special trickery in fighting was recurrent in literature.

With the two passages above, Milton was probably familiar. His poetic soul sensed the appropriateness and effectiveness of the comparison in each instance. But, Milton-like, when he came to write his own version, he made several significant changes. While describing Satan's ignominious return to Hell, his expecting to get a glorious reception and instead finding that his followers have turned tail and fled into deeper hell, the poet can think of no better analogy than that with the deceitful Tartar:

> As when the *Tartar* from his *Russian* Foe
> By *Astracan* over the Snowie Plaines
> Retires (Bk. x, ll. 431-433).

[44] *Faerie Queene*, II, xi, 26, 6-8.   [45] *Poetical Works*, II, 150.

53

Milton has altered Spenser's "by the Caspian lake" and Fletcher's "by Russian Volgha's frozen banks" into "By *Astracan*," and by this mention of a specific city has succeeded in objectifying his whole description. Furthermore, and this is significant too, "Astracan" has its own poetic value.

There have been several conjectures why that particular city should have been chosen. Verity[46] cites the opening sentence of *A Brief History*, which mentions the Tartars and Astracan. But nothing is even suggested there about warfare. Gilbert[47] is much more apt to be right when he quotes two passages from Hakluyt. Both passages refer, not merely to Astracan and the Tartars, but to Russo-Tartar warfare as well. It is, however, only the second one which Gilbert says "is probably one of the sources of *P.L.* 10. 431-3." This appears the less likely because it is in the account of the Bannister-Ducket voyage into Persia,[48] whereas the first passage is derived from the very pages of Jenkinson's narrative with which we know Milton worked. But another short paragraph[49] in those same pages seems to have an even better chance of being "the source":

All the countrey upon our right hand the river Volga, from over against the river Cama unto the towne of Astracan, is the land of Crimme [in the margin, The Crimme Tartars], whose inhabitants be also of the lawe of Mahomet, and live for the most part according to the fashions of the Nagayes, having continual wars with the Emperour of Russia.

If we can assume that Milton took his own advice as given in *A Brief History* and read the whole of Fletcher's *Russe Common Wealth*, another passage should be quoted as pertinent here. We need not assume even that he read all

---

[46] *Op.cit.*, p. 600.   [47] *Op.cit.*, pp. 36-37.

[48] See Hakluyt, *op.cit.*, III, 150-151. Cf. also L. C. Tihany, PQ, XIII (1934), 305-306.

[49] *Ibid.*, II, 453. See also *Early Voyages*, vol. I, 53, 57, 58. In all three cases the Russo-Tartar warfare is mentioned in close conjunction with Astracan.

of Fletcher since the part in question is printed in Hakluyt's selection;[50] in a section headed "Of the Tartars, and other borderers to the country of Russia, with whom they have most to doe in warre, and peace," occurs the following:

> The principall cause of this continual quarell betwixt the Russe and the Chrim is for the right of certaine border partes claimed by the Tartar, but possessed by the Russe. The Tartar alleageth that besides Astracan and Cazan (that are the ancient posses-sion of the East Tartar) the whole countrey from his bounds North and Westward so farre as the citie of Mosko, and Mosko it selfe perteineth to his right.

One aspect of Milton's lines has not received sufficient notice. Wherever he could, the poet surrounded Satan and his followers with an atmosphere of deceptiveness. One of the characteristics most often associated with Tartars in Milton's day was their deceptiveness in fighting. The trick-ery as Phineas Fletcher gives it in the lines quoted above was known at least since Polo's time.[51] Giles Fletcher him-self, on the very page just quoted where he describes Russo-Tartar warfare, says of the latter: "They are very expert horsemen, and use to shoote as readily backward, as for-ward." And he devotes the next two pages to "the subtiltie of the Tartar." The tradition was indeed so strong[52] that Milton could count on his readers' making the proper asso-ciation.

Another passage in that same Tenth Book depends simi-larly on his audience's comprehension of the background. Actually the background is largely given in *A Brief History*. Though that work professes to be a compendious history of Russia, it is really little more than Russia as seen through English eyes; it is indeed the "Relations of Moscovia, As far as hath been discover'd by English Voyages." And even a casual reader cannot help noticing the recurrent note of

---

[50] See *op.cit.*, III, 390-391.　　[51] See *The Book*, I, 262-263.
[52] For the frequency with which the trait was referred to, cf. R. R. Cawley, *The Voyagers and Elizabethan Drama*, p. 201.

nationalism. What the English had accomplished Milton was justly proud of, and his pride is both explicit and implicit in what he says. Russia's fine buildings are the less fine in comparison with British. Russian religion is virtually paganism contrasted with English protestantism. But clearly Milton's chief interest is in the trail-blazers, notably Sir Hugh Willoughby, and Chancelor, and Anthony Jenkinson. He reserves for them the last and crucial chapter, the one that begins with such a proud flourish, "The discovery of *Russia* by the northern Ocean, made first, of any Nation that we know, by *English* men, might have seem'd an enterprise almost heroick."

Today we are scarcely aware of how the project of a Northeast Passage to Cathay possessed English minds during the last half of the sixteenth century until its feasibility had been largely disproved. "There was never," wrote Richard Eden,[53] "any more woorthy commendation and admiration then is that whiche owre nation have attempted by the north seas to discover the mightie and riche empire of Cathay." It was not merely Willoughby's experience but the cases of his successors as well which kept the whole matter in such prominence. There is something tragic in the careful instructions handed to adventurers at their departure; part of the commission (1580) to Pet and Jackman read as follows:[54]

The said Governours, and company [Muscovy Company] have hired the saide Arthur Pet.... And likewise the said Charles Jackman . . . for a voyage by them to be made by Gods grace, for search and discoveries of a passage by sea from hence by Boroughs streights, and the Island Vaigats, Eastwards, to the countreis or dominions of the mightie Prince, the Emperour of Cathay. . . . We hope that the continent or firme land of Asia doth not stretch it selfe so farre Northwards, but that there may

[53] *First Three English Books on America*, p. 59.
[54] Hakluyt, *op.cit.*, III, 252-254.
The famous John Dee was asked for and freely gave his advice on the northeastern discovery. See Hakluyt, *op.cit.*, III, 262-263.

be found a sea passeable by it. . . . Passe Eastwards alongst the same coast, keeping it alwayes in your sight . . . untill you come to the mouth of the river Ob . . . and being in sight of the same Easterly land, doe you in Gods name proceed alongst by it, from thence Eastwards . . . untill you come to the Countrey of Cathay.[55]

Like all the rest, this voyage was turned back because of the impenetrable ice en route. In fact, the whole narrative fairly shivers with ice.[56] And after years of stubborn heroism, loss of life, and endurance beyond belief, the British were finally driven to acknowledge that their Northeast Passage was but a mockery. The seventeenth century was barely half over when Milton's Heylyn[57] was to say resignedly: "The undertaking is unprofitable, the successe impossible."

In light of all this Milton's lines acquire particular significance. While he is impressing us with the terrible depredations of Sin and Death, released from their infernal dungeon upon a doomed world, he resorts to this memorable comparison:

> As when two Polar Winds blowing adverse
> Upon the *Cronian* Sea, together drive
> Mountains of Ice, that stop th' imagin'd way
> Beyond *Petsora* Eastward, to the rich
> *Cathaian* Coast (Bk. x, ll. 289-293).[58]

[55] Cf. also the 15th item in the Russia Company's Articles to her merchants in Muscovy (Hakluyt, *op.cit.*, II, 285): "That you use all wayes and meanes possible to learne howe men may passe from Russia, either by land or by sea to Cathaia." How important the English considered the whole matter may be seen by the active part the ancient and tried Sebastian Cabot was induced to play in the project. See Hakluyt, *op.cit.*, II, 239, 240; III, 331.

[56] Cf. Hakluyt, *op.cit.*, III, 282-303.

[57] *Cosmographie*, II, 161. The "Table" (1670) lists "North-East passage," then "North-West passage" with the comment "little probability of doing any good in either."

[58] How impressed Milton was with the insuperable difficulties of the Cathay voyage is shown in his having used the same figure in *Areopagitica*; he says there that the contagion of foreign books "will finde a passage to the people farre easier and shorter than an Indian voyage, though it

"Th' imagin'd way" takes on special poignancy.[59] And
it is interesting to observe how, with the mention of "Petsora," Milton has succeeded in objectifying the passage precisely as he did with "Astracan." Why, however, did he
choose particularly *Petsora*? The word occurs several times
in *A Brief History*. Especially it occurs in connection with
the "certain Merchants of Hull," who can be identified
from the source as William Gourdon and his party.[60] In
Purchas[61] it is given as "A Voyage made to Pechora 1611.
Written by William Gourdon of Hull, appointed chiefe
Pilot." This narrative[62] if anything contains more ice than
the Pet-Jackman: "We weighed, and . . . came safely over
the Barre of Pechora. From thence wee directed our course
for Nova Zembla: and at noone we came to Ice. . . . The
second being very cleere, and seeing no way to passe to the
Northward for Ice, we determined to return." And these
are by his own admission the very pages Milton was working through for his *Brief History of Moscovia*. Among the

---

could be sail'd either by the North of *Cataio* Eastward, or of *Canada* Westward" (*Works*, IV, 313).

[59] On "th' imagin'd way," see Hakluyt, *op.cit.*, II, 241, "whereas yet it
was doubtfull whether there were any passage yea or no," in a passage we
know Milton used for his *History of Moscovia*.

On the preceding "drive Mountains of Ice," see Hakluyt, *op.cit.*, II, 244,
"the way would bee stopt and bard by the force of the Ice," in another
passage we know Milton used. And Purchas (*Pilgrimes* [1625], III, 527)
used the very words: "Neither hereafter will I marvell, though the Streight
of Waygats bee stopped up to the North-east, with such huge Mountaines
of Ice."

On "rich *Cathaian* Coast," cf. Hakluyt, *op.cit.*, II, 398, "to passe the
sayde Seas to discover Cataia . . . by the riches that might bee brought
from thence. And also (*ibid.*, II, 481): "this land of Cathay . . . unspeake-
ably rich." But of course Cathay's riches were something of a commonplace.

[60] See my edition of the History, *Milton's Literary Craftsmanship*, Princeton, 1941, pp. 13 and 50.

[61] *Op.cit.*, XIII, 194.

[62] Purchas, *op.cit.*, XIII, 203. Cf. also from the same voyage *ibid.*, XIII,
199: "In the morning the Ice came so extreamely upon us, that we could
not weigh; for our men being cast from the Capstan, our Cable brake, and
so wee lost an Anchor. Then seeing wee could not passe to the Eastward,
wee stood to the Westward of Cape Swetinos."

acknowledged sources at the end is "Gourdon *of* Hull's *Voiage to* Pechora." One of the details Milton[63] here reproduces from Gourdon's account is that the River Pechora is "full of Ice." Right after Gourdon's story in Purchas[64] comes a letter of Richard Finch telling of the same ill-fated expedition. In it Finch writes: "Wee came to the mouth of the River of Pechora. . . . And being entred into the aforesaid Harbour, it was full of Ice, and hard to finde." From there[65] they directed their course "for Nova Zembla, till that wee had runne so farre, and were so inclosed in huge Ice, that in a Day and a Night we could goe neither backward nor forward: And finding no means to proceed on our intended Voyage for Nova Zembla, wee cleared our selves out of that place." There is ample evidence that Milton used the Finch letter in his *History*. After Finch in Purchas[66] appears "The Voyage of Master Josias Logan to Pechora." Among his sources Milton lists "Josias Logan." And following Logan, Purchas[67] prints "A briefe Relation of a Voyage to Pechora, and wintering there . . . by William Pursglove." Once more Milton acknowledges "*The Voiage* of William Pursglove, *to* Pechora." It is hardly any wonder that with all this emphasis the poet should have chosen "Petsora"[68] as the bleak, eerie, frigid background for Sin and Death.

[63] *Works*, x, 332. Gilbert (*op.cit.*, p. 308) quotes the passage, about the "Streight of Waygats," which has the actual expression, "Mountaines of Ice" (see Purchas, *op.cit.*, XIII, 187).

[64] *Op.cit.*, XIII, 205.

[65] *Ibid.*, XIII, 209.

[66] *Op.cit.*, XIII, 222ff. Here too ice is emphasized: "The frost was so strong, that the Ozera was frozen over, and the Ice driving in the River to and againe, brake all the nets" (p. 226).

[67] *Op.cit.*, XIII, 239ff.

[68] On the spelling, Milton in the *History* gives "*Pechora* or *Petzora*" (*Works*, x, 332). His acknowledged source at this point has "Pechora" (see Purchas, *op.cit.*, XIII, 201-203). Hakluyt has both "Pechora" and "Petzora" (see *op.cit.*, II, 327-341 and III, 405-412). For what it may be worth, Purchas (XIII, 180) also has "Petsora," exactly Milton's spelling.

There is one final point which concerns the Northeast Passage. If, as has often been contended, Milton chose to see something of Cromwell in the early Satan who still retains a portion of his heroic mould, it is quite conceivable that he might have seen in him some of the other national heroes. The English critic may have spoken better than he knew when he wrote[69] that Milton "is the only poet of his age who has not forgotten the sublime adventurers of the previous century." There is no question, for instance, that he was deeply impressed with Sir Hugh Willoughby.[70] One need read only that fifth chapter of *A Brief History* to sense his admiration. He follows Sir Hugh's career straight through: his choice as admiral, his marshaling of the fleet, his discipline, his great courage, his intelligent meeting of adverse circumstances, his death at *"Arzina* in *Lapland* neer to *Kegor,"* the discovery of his body by Russian fishermen the following year, the body's being sent back home by an English agent; and he even describes the sinking of the funeral ship on its voyage to England. These are quite a few details to include about one man in a fifty-page History of Russia. It is further noticeable that *"The Journal of Sir* Hugh Willowby" occurs first in Milton's own list of sources. Third in this same list is *"Another* [discourse] *of* Clement Adams *taken from the mouth of* Chancelor." We know that Milton followed Adams' account closely and in detail.[71] And it is that narrative which reminds us at points of the famous council scene in Pandemonium where the "heroic" Satan volunteers to undertake the hazardous voyage to

[69] See "Milton and India," TLS, April 6, 1933, p. 248.

[70] The only place where I have seen this suggestion developed is in an article by H. Mutschmann, "Studies Concerning the Origin of 'Paradise Lost,'" Dorpat, 1924. The suggestion is there overlaid with so much material which the majority of scholars will hesitate to accept as to be almost buried. Furthermore, what seem to me the most important connections are not drawn. Mutschmann has another short pamphlet (eight pages) *Milton in Russland*, Dorpat, 1924. My own conclusions were drawn and formulated before I had seen Mutschmann's proposal.

[71] See R. R. Cawley, *Milton's Literary Craftsmanship*, p. 15.

earth and so to open up a new way for his companions;[72]
Beelzebub speaks the words of introduction:

> But first whom shall we send
> In search of this new world, whom shall we find
> Sufficient? who shall tempt with wandring feet
> The dark unbottom'd infinite Abyss
> And through the palpable obscure find out
> His uncouth way, ...
> . . . . what strength, what art can then
> Suffice . . . .
> . . . . . . Here he had need
> All circumspection, and wee now no less
> Choice in our suffrage; for on whom we send,
> The weight of all and our last hope relies.
> This said, he sat; and expectation held
> His look suspence, awaiting who appeer'd
> To second, or oppose, or undertake
> The perilous attempt; but all sat mute,
> Pondering the danger with deep thoughts; and each
> In others count'nance red his own dismay
> Astonisht: none among the choice and prime
> Of those Heav'n-warring Champions could be found
> So hardie as to proffer or accept
> Alone the dreadful voyage; till at last
> *Satan*, whom now transcendent glory rais'd
> Above his fellows, with Monarchal pride
> Conscious of highest worth, unmov'd thus spake.
> O Progeny of Heav'n, Empyreal Thrones,
> With reason hath deep silence and demurr
> Seis'd us, though undismaid: long is the way
> And hard . . . .
> If thence he scape into what ever world,
> Or unknown Region, what remains him less
> Then unknown dangers and as hard escape.
> But I should ill become this Throne . . . .
> . . . . if aught propos'd
> And judg'd of public moment, in the shape
> Of difficulty or danger could deterre
> Me from attempting (Bk. ii, ll. 402-450).

[72] In a separate article I hope to show how Milton has consistently thought of Satan's journey from beginning to end as a typical voyage.

In the Adams narrative[73] when the northeast project was broached "to open a way and passage to our men for travaile to newe and unknowen kingdomes,"

in this so hard and difficult a matter, they first make choyse of certaine grave and wise persons in maner of a Senate or companie, which should lay their heads together, and give their judgements. . . .

Sufficient Captaines and governours of so great an enterprise were as yet wanting: to which office and place, although many men, (and some voyde of experience) offered themselves, yet one Sir Hugh Willoughbie a most valiant Gentleman, and well borne, very earnestly requested to have that care and charge committed unto him: of whom before all others, both by reason of his goodly personage (for he was of a tall stature) as also for his singular skill in the services of warre, the company of the Marchants made greatest accompt: so that at the last they concluded and made choyce of him for the Generall of this voyage, and appoynted to him the Admirall with authoritie and commaund over all the rest.[74]

Another part of the Adams account with which Milton was obviously impressed, a part which follows immediately after the above, was Henry Sidney's eloquent proposal[75] that Richard Chancelor be one to accompany Willoughby in a position of great importance. Milton[76] speaks of Sidney's "coming where the Adventurers were gather'd together" and of the "grave and eloquent Speech" with which he commended Chancelor. In this speech, referred to by Milton in *A Brief History*, Sidney reminded the company,

into howe many perils for your sakes, and his countreys love, he is nowe to runne: whereof it is requisite that wee be not un-

---

[73] See Hakluyt, *op.cit.*, II, 240-243. A considerable amount of material from these pages is reproduced by Milton in *A Brief History*.
[74] No one familiar with the Willoughby narratives can help being reminded of the experience of Satan's followers:

> Beyond this flood a frozen Continent
> Lies dark and wilde, beat with perpetual storms
> Of Whirlwind and dire Hail, which on firm land
> Thaws not, but gathers heap, and ruin seems
> Of ancient pile; all else deep snow and ice (Bk. II, ll. 587-591).

[75] See Hakluyt, *op.cit.*, II, 242-243.   [76] *Works*, X, 365.

mindefull, if it please God to send him good successe. . . . He commits his life (a thing to a man of all things most deare) to the raging Sea, and the uncertainties of many dangers. We shall here live and rest at home quietly with our friends. . . . We shall keepe our owne coastes and countrey: Hee shall seeke strange and unknowen kingdomes. . . . Wherefore in respect of the greatnesse of the dangers, and the excellencie of his charge, you are to favour and love the man thus departing from us: and if it fall so happily out that hee returne againe it is your part and duetie also, liberally to reward him.

After that this noble yong Gentleman had delivered this or some such like speech, much more eloquently then I can possiblie report it, the companie then present beganne one to looke upon another, one to question and conferre with another: and some (to whom the vertue and sufficiencie of the man was knowen) began secretly to rejoyce with themselves, and to conceive a speciall hope, that the man would proove in time very rare and excellent. . . . After all this, the companie growing to some silence. . . .[77]

It is not too much to read here also Satan's reminding his followers of their comparatively soft life at home during his absence,

> intend at home,
> While here shall be our home (ll. 457-458),

and his insistence that he willingly accepts the dangers though he expects to be honored in return,

> as great a share
> Of hazard as of honour (ll. 452-453).[78]

[77] This whole passage is from the section in Hakluyt already referred to (II, 242-243).

[78] Another passage which Milton may also have had in mind occurs within four pages of this: "And as hee [Chancelor] was preparing himselfe to depart [from Wardhouse in Norway], it happened that hee fell in company and speech with certaine Scottishmen: who having understanding of his intention, and wishing well to his actions, beganne earnestly to disswade him from the further prosecution of the discoverie, by amplifying the dangers which hee was to fall into, and omitted no reason that might serve to that purpose. But hee holding nothing so ignominious and reprochfull, as inconstancie and levitie of minde, and perswading himselfe that a man of valour coulde not commit a more dishonourable part then for feare of danger to avoyde and shunne great attempts, was nothing at all changed or discouraged with the speeches and words of the Scots, remaining stedfast

From the foregoing it is reasonable to assume that Milton's knowledge of Russia as shown in *Paradise Lost* was gained almost exclusively in that period, possibly just before 1650, when he was studying Hakluyt and Purchas with the purpose of digesting their materials for his little compendium. He formed then certain general impressions of the country which were largely confirmed in his capacity as government secretary. When some ten years later he came to write his great epic, he saw the chance to use some of that knowledge in striking figures whose significance his intelligent countrymen would fully understand. Some of those figures, as we have seen, are based on general and slightly prejudiced impressions. Others have in them specific references which make one assume that here too the amanuenses were being used to reread to him certain passages which he had read "with some delight" back in those happier days "before he lost his sight."[79]

---

and immutable in his first resolution: determining either to bring that to passe which was intended, or els to die the death." (Hakluyt, *op.cit.*, II, 247.) Here again it is reasonable to discern the great dangers confronting Satan, his firm resolution, his contempt for weakness, his stern injunction to Beelzebub: "Fall'n Cherube, to be weak is miserable."

[79] Quite a little has been written about Milton's spelling of "Ksar" (Bk. XI, l. 394). Some light on the question may be thrown by a quotation from his *Brief History*: "The great Dukes of *Muscovy* derive their Pedegree, though without ground, from *Augustus Caesar*" (*Works*, X, 348). But it should also be noticed that Spenser has "kesars" and "keasars" (see *F.Q.*, II, vii, 5, 9; III, xi, 29, 9; IV, vii, 1, 4; V, ix, 29, 9; VI, iii, 5, 7; VI, xii, 28, 7). For Spenser it was a convenient alliterative with "king."

CHAPTER IV

MILTON'S TRADITIONALISM

IT IS hardly surprising, in light of Milton's training and education, that his early poems should contain so many geographical references which are traditionally classical and Biblical. We know from Phillips' account how from tender years he studied the Bible, how he followed the guidance of Thomas Young, who turned "this way and that the massive scrolls of the Fathers of old, or the Holy Books of the one true God"; we know what St. Paul's under Alexander Gill was like, what stress the Cambridge of those days laid on the classics, what Horton did to strengthen and confirm in the maturing poet that deep knowledge. We should never overlook, furthermore, that Milton was bred in a tradition which virtually demanded that examples should be cited from the ancients. Even if he had not independently learned the importance of such citation, that sage and serious master Spenser must have taught him to imitate what in *Areopagitica*[1] he was to call "the old and elegant humanity of Greece." Naturally too the very language in which so many of the early poems were written called for Latin references; we should not underestimate how the classical imagery of *In Quintum Novembris* may have permeated *Lycidas* and *Comus* and even *L'Allegro*.

The tendency of all this would be to make Milton seek his examples from the great who were of old. When, therefore, we find him choosing his instances of free commonwealths from ancient times;[2] when we find him deriving from Aristotle, Plato, Virgil, Ovid, and Martial all his examples of logical principles, we should have our impression confirmed. The girls with whom he compares[3] the more favored English ones are not French or Italian or Spanish,

[1] *Works*, IV, 295.   [2] In *The Ready and Easy Way.*
[3] First Latin Elegy. See *Poetical Works*, p. 564.

but those of "Achaemenia," or in "Memnon's Nineveh," the maidens of Troy and Greece and Rome. It is the same with foreign countries in general. Egypt and Ethiopia, Arabia and India manage largely to retain their reputations which had been set centuries before.

Egypt is a particularly good case in point. Gilbert[4] is quite right in saying that "Milton's references to Egypt are almost all dependent on the Bible, and many of them figurative." In the Nativity Ode he refers to the traditional Egyptian gods:

> The brutish gods of *Nile* as fast,
> *Isis* and *Orus*, and the Dog *Anubis* hast.
> Nor is *Osiris* seen
> In *Memphian* Grove, or Green (ll. 211-214).[5]

The next line,

Trampling the unshowr'd Grasse with lowings loud (l. 215),

with its reference to Egypt's lack of rain, introduces an element with which we will become very familiar. Milton was certainly aware, from his readings in the classics, that Egypt's parched soil was dependent on periodic overflowings of the Nile. At the same time, there is every evidence that he knew George Sandys' popular *Relation of a Journey begun An. Dom. 1610* (1615). And Sandys had written: "The earth then burnt with the violent fervour, never refreshed with Rain, (which here falls rarely, and then only in the Winter) hath help from Nilus."[6] This matter of using a modern traveler to bring up to date, so to speak, traditional material came with Milton to be virtually a practice. Clearly this is what he has done with the pyramids:

[4] *Geog. Dict.*, p. 111.
[5] He repeats three of these in *Paradise Lost*, I, 478. Such gods appear also in the prose. See *Works*, III, 173; IV, 338.
   The allusions to locusts in the first book (ll. 341-342) and last (l. 185) of *Paradise Lost* are of course purely Biblical.
[6] Quoted by Gilbert, *op.cit.*, p. 187. Fuller (*Pisgah-Sight*, Bk. IV, 79) wrote of Egypt: "Rain is very rare in this land (and that onely in winter)."

And here let those
Who boast in mortal things, and wondring tell
Of *Babel*, and the works of *Memphian* Kings,
Learn how thir greatest Monuments of Fame,
And Strength and Art are easily outdone
By Spirits reprobate, and in an hour
What in an age they with incessant toyle
And hands innumerable scarce perform (Bk. 1, ll. 692-699).

He undoubtedly knew Pliny's elaborate account of the many workmen enslaved to erect the huge piles. But the special philosophy underlying the passage, wherein the vain shows of men are placed below even Pandemonium, may well have been suggested by Sandys:[7] "Full West of the City, ... stand those three Pyramides (the barbarous Monuments of prodigality and vainglory) so universally celebrated." Sandys' translation[8] from Martial,

Of her Pyramides let Memphis bost
No more, the barbarous wonders of vaine cost,

would tend also to confirm the impression in Milton's mind. On the other hand, it is unlikely that an author like John Greaves would have contributed anything to the poet.[9] And neither does Leo Africanus contribute anything of importance from his *History and Description of Africa*.

Ethiopia played a role similar to Egypt's. Necessarily Milton would use somewhere the age-old proverb, so popular with the dramatists, "to wash an Ethiope," doubtless Biblical in origin. In *Pro Se Defensio*[10] he excoriates More in claim-

[7] Quoted by Gilbert, *op.cit.*, p. 188. Verity (*op.cit.*, p. 395) quotes an apt passage from Jonson's *Prince Henry's Barriers*.

[8] *Relation* (1621 ed.), p. 132. Also quoted by Gilbert.

[9] Greaves was the professor of Astronomy at Oxford, and his *Pyramidographia* (1646) was too technical for Milton's purposes. He is, for example, too much interested in exact measurements to be philosophical. As one instance, he writes (*op.cit.*, p. 94) that the length of a certain chamber "is thirty four English feet, and 300 and 80 parts of the foot divided into a thousand (that is 34 feet and 380 of 1000 parts of a foot)." And with professorial accuracy he delights to correct Sandys' blunders.

[10] *Works*, IX, 255. See also *ibid.*, III, 414 (from *The Doctrine and Discipline*).

ing that "Riverius, by washing you, whitened an Ethiopian and expended his labour and chalk to no purpose." And as might also be expected, he uses the term in the traditional sense of "black,"[11] once more perhaps because it had been popular with the dramatists, especially with Shakespeare. Other allusions, however, involve us in more controversy. Describing Satan making his tortuous way up through the mirk of hell, Milton can think of no better simile than that of an East Indian fleet:

> they on the trading Flood
> Through the wide *Ethiopian* to the Cape
> Ply stemming nightly toward the Pole (Bk. ii, ll. 640-642).

In this passage the poet clearly visualizes the Ethiopian Sea as being on the east of Africa. But the cartographers were in no such blissful state of certainty. Verity[12] points to Milton's mistake since on most maps he finds the Sea between Africa and South America, and he cites specifically Hexham's Mercator and Heylyn. But even here there was no real consistency. The latter,[13] for example, classifies among his "Aethiopick Islands" those which are *east* of Africa. The disagreement goes back to the Ancients, who themselves were vague about the whole matter. In classical times "Ethiopian" was a term often used to embrace the entire southern ocean as then known. Before Milton's day, however, it had been moved west, and the most reputable atlases showed it between Africa and South America.[14] Ethel Seaton[15] in her brilliant essay, "Marlowe's Map," has

[11] See *Works*, xii, 131. In *Prolusions*.

[12] See *Paradise Lost*, pp. 417-418.

[13] *Microcosmos* (1636), p. 1000. This matter is repeated in *Cosmographie*, iv, 83-84. In his map of Africa, on the other hand, Heylyn places the sea conspicuously on the west. Purchas, in one passage at least, has it on the east. See Gilbert, *op.cit.*, p. 119.

[14] See A. E. Nordenskiöld, Facsimile-Atlas, Stockholm, 1889, Map xlvi (Ortelius, 1570), Map xlvii (Mercator, 1587), Map xlviii (Cornelius De Judaeis, 1593).

[15] See *Essays and Studies by Members of the English Association*, x (1924), 17.

fully proved that when Marlowe makes Techelles represent "the Ethiopian sea" as being viewed from "the Westerne part of Affricke" he was not merely making no mistake but was following the best cartographic authority of his day, Ortelius.

It can be reasoned that Milton, whose passion for maps is well known, would normally have accepted the best authorities of his time and would have used some other term to describe his fleet "close sailing from *Bengala*" and making its way arduously towards the Cape of Hope. It can further be argued that since he had doubtless been blind for years before he composed this particular passage, his mind might have reverted to the classical conception with which he had earlier been familiar. Another way to look at it, and the more likely, is that he recalled both theories, and that "wide *Ethiopian* to the Cape" struck him as being a felicitous combination of sounds, as it certainly is.

There is only one other passage in which the poet used Ethiopia; in this instance, however, Milton is reflecting primarily the work of a modern traveler. The passage occurs in the fourth book where he is at pains to seek comparisons with Eve's beautiful garden in Paradise:

> Nor where *Abassin* Kings thir issue Guard,
> Mount *Amara*, though this by som suppos'd
> True Paradise under the *Ethiop* Line
> By *Nilus* head, enclos'd with shining Rock,
> A whole dayes journey high (ll. 280-284).

This is another of those passages which have caused perhaps unnecessary controversy. Scholars have wavered between Purchas and Heylyn in giving main credit for the lines. G. W. Whiting[16] adds Ortelius. But surely Todd[17] was right in his original conjecture that here we have Heylyn.

[16] *Milton's Literary Milieu*, p. 110.
[17] Todd strangely missed one of the most important parts of the comparison.

In a passage to which attention is clearly called through large print at mid-page, "Amara," Heylyn[18] writes:

The chief City of it called *Amara* by the name of the Province, situate in the midst of the Empire; and though not much distant from the *Aequator*, if not plainly under it, yet blessed with such a temperate air, such a fruitful soyl, such ravishing pleasures of all sorts, that some have taken (but mistaken) it for the place of *Paradise*: So strangely Heaven, Earth, Nature, and Humane industry have joyned their helps together to enrich and beautifie it. But that which is the greatest Ornament of this Province, and indeed of the whole Empire of *Aethiopia*, is the Mountain *Amara*, situate in a large and delightful Plain: the bottom of the Hill in circuit 90 miles, and *a dayes journey high* [my italics]; the Rock so smooth and even (but lesser and lesser towards the top) that no wall can be more evenly polished . . . : the Plain . . . honoured with 34 Palaces, in which the younger sons of the *Emperour* are continually inclosed, to avoid sedition.

Here is every element for Milton's description, and it is the only passage which contains every element. Purchas, for example, does not have the "dayes journey high." And Lane Cooper's proposal[19] that the *Pilgrimage* is the real source is therefore probably wrong. If we add to the above the evidence of the maps, it makes the case still more likely. Heylyn's "Africa" shows the equator going straight through Mount Amara. Furthermore, his spelling is "Abassine,"[20] and the inscription reads: "In the Hill Amara the sons of the Emperour of Aethiopia are held Inward or kept by a garrison." Only, the way it is printed on the map, the "garrison," part of which is printed on a separate line, looks very much like "guard." It would have been easy for an amanuensis to misread the word.

[18] *Cosmographie* (1652), Bk. IV, 64. E. M. Clark's "Milton's Abyssinian Paradise" (University of Texas *Studies in English*, XXIX, 129-150) appeared after the present volume had been submitted for publication.

[19] *Mod. Philol.*, III, 327ff. McColley (*Paradise Lost*, p. 157), Gilbert (*op.cit.*, pp. 18-20), and Whiting (*op.cit.*, pp. 110-111) all quote Purchas. And so, as it happens, does Todd.

[20] See *op.cit.*, IV, 63 and 59.

Perhaps the best example of all of Milton's traditionalism is to be found with Arabia. From ancient times that country was thought of as being divided into three parts, Petraea, Deserta, or Felix (Pliny); the last part was the most often referred to and it was regularly associated with balms, gums, and incense; it was furthermore made the home of the unique and perennial phoenix. Through such entrenched traditionalism the poet makes virtually no breach. And it is significant that the Arabian references do not essentially differ from beginning to end. The "desertas Arabum" appear in Elegy iv,[21] the "deserts of Arabia" in the *Apology*,[22] and "Arabian drouth" in *Paradise Regained*.[23] It is the same with Arabia Felix; the fragrance permeates Milton's verse from "anno aetatis 20" until "that self-begott'n bird" revives in the last hundred lines of what is possibly his final poetic work. For some reason the poet deliberately chose not to "modernize." After the country's fragrance there is perhaps no quality so often insisted on in contemporary literature as the thieving nature of its inhabitants. Heylyn[24] was only one of many to emphasize this characteristic when he described them as "living for the most part upon spoil and robberie, as all that travell that way know by sad experience." For all the commonness of this reputation,[25] there is no mention of it in Milton.

There is only one passage that falls even slightly out of picture:

> As when to them who sail
> Beyond the *Cape of Hope*, and now are past
> *Mozambic*, off at Sea North-East windes blow
> *Sabean* Odours from the spicie shoare
> Of *Arabie* the blest (Bk. iv, ll. 159-163).

It is customary to trace these lines to Diodorus.[26] Verity

[21] L. 99.   [22] *Works*, iii, 352.   [23] Bk. iii, l. 274.
[24] *Cosmographie*, iii, 111.
[25] See R. R. Cawley, *Voyagers and Elizabethan Drama*, pp. 178-181.
[26] Cf. Verity's *Paradise Lost*, pp. 455-456; Gilbert, *op.cit.*, pp. 27-28;

rightly calls attention to the fact that the description in his History "is removed only a few chapters from that account of Ammon and Amalthea which was the undoubted source of 275-79." But it was a common experience for sailors to smell the fragrance of Arabia while far away and to comment on their enjoyment.[27] If, however, a book source must be found, Diodorus is as good as any. One more element that has drawn comment on the above lines is Milton's "mistake" in making the wind blow at "North-East." Verity, for example, commented: "rather *north*, according to modern geography." It is easy enough to do for Milton what Seaton did for Marlowe. Here Masson, in defense of his master, has the right of it. Many contemporary maps show Mozambique distinctly southwest of Arabia, so that "north" would have been positively wrong. Heylyn, for instance, in his map of Africa proves that ships which are "past *Mozambic*" would depend on northeasterly breezes if they were to enjoy the fragrance of Arabia Felix.[28] Geographic accuracy is not necessary in poetry; but a poet in 1660 could hardly have done better than to follow the authority of Heylyn.

There is naturally much traditional material which, because of its associational value, a poet refuses to let go. It does not matter that later travelers have proved the untruth of it; it does not matter even if the poet knows they have proved the untruth of it. Especially in the case of a poet like Milton such material, through early training and association, becomes so much a part of him that he uses it with-

---

Thompson, SP, XVI, 162; Whiting, *op.cit.*, pp. 68-69. The last-named adds Ortelius. See pp. 118-119.

[27] An earlier reflection in literature is to be seen in Lodge's *Margarite of America* (*Complete Wks.*, III, 45); the ladies in attendance on Margarite are shown dispensing from censers "most pleasant odours, such as in the pride of the yeare breath along the coast of Arabia Faelix."

[28] This is almost equally true of Ortelius (see Nordenskiöld, Map XLVI) and Mercator (*ibid.*, Map XLVII).

out second thought. He no more hesitates to use old geography than he hesitated to use old astronomy after he felt sure Ptolemy was wrong. Here as well Spenser had his influence. Milton had too deep a respect for his native language,

> that by sinews weak
> Didst move my first endeavouring tongue to speak,

to archaize his words. But archaizing may just as well be applied to material, and there is an abundance of it in his poetry. When one gathers together all the stereotyped classical expressions, one is amazed that Milton's verse, especially his early verse, can remain so fresh in its impression. Cimmerian darkness, cold Olympus, Libyan sands, golden Tagus, snowy Alp, Caspian tiger, Libyan lions, Orion armed, smooth Adonis, rocks of Caucasus, warlike Scythian, Lydian airs, sandy Ladon, Trachinian cliff, Aonian mount —all these make him sound like a Latin poet writing in English, or at least in Latin-English.

This tendency then extends itself to certain expressions which give us the impression that Milton cannot be an English poet writing in the seventeenth century. England herself is an outpost "on the western frontiers of the world!"[29] And London is a "city reared by Dardan settlers."[30] In the same way Spain is "the Hesperian land,"[31] and even Italy remains "th' *Hesperian* Fields."[32] Because Juvenal made the Orcades (Orkney) one limit of the known world, Milton writes of "the farthest Orcades"[33] though *ultima Thule* had long since been moved to Iceland and beyond. When in the First Defense[34] he seeks instances of tyranny he finds them in early Persian history in spite of there being supreme examples from Russia, which by that

---

[29] *In Quintum Novembris*, l. 157. See MacKellar, *op.cit.*, p. 129.
[30] *Elegia prima*, l. 73. See *Works*, I, 175.
[31] *Elegia tertia*, l. 46. See *Works*, I, 183.
[32] *P.L.*, Bk. I, l. 520.
[33] *Second Defense*. See *Works*, VIII, 235.   [34] *Works*, VII, 301ff.

time he knew so well. In fact, there seems something almost deliberate in his avoidance of the Russian example. Egyptian tyranny occurs in *The Reason of Church Government*,[35] and Turkish tyranny is alluded to with some frequency in such works as *Prolusions*,[36] *Eikonoklastes*,[37] and the Commonplace Book.[38] Furthermore, he lays considerable emphasis on Spanish tyranny over the Indians in the Declaration against Spain.[39] But though he had written in *A Brief History of Moscovia*[40] that "the Emperour exerciseth absolute power" and had in his researches read numerous instances of the Czar's overlordship, one looks in vain through the other works for references to Russian tyranny.[41]

There is another consideration which might have influenced Milton to use the traditional material. A poet may well feel that the introduction of a "modern" reference might strike directly across the mood he is trying to create. *Paradise Lost* contains more than its share of such contemporary allusions or suggestions. But at other times Milton quite deliberately refrained from introducing what might be construed as an intrusive element. What this usually means is that the connection with something current, which would make the picture perhaps even more effective to the ordinary reader, is quite deliberately not made. For all we know, this may be a part of his choosing to appeal to the fit audience though few. At any rate it is not difficult to observe the theory in practice. The Fortunate Isles were

[35] *Works*, III, 222.   [36] *Ibid.*, XII, 271.

[37] *Ibid.*, v, 282 and 283.

[38] *Ibid.*, XVIII, 184. Note also Articles of Peace, *ibid.*, VI, 253.

[39] Cf. particularly *ibid.*, XIII, 513, 515, 527, 551. Masson doubted that the pamphlet was Milton's, but the Columbia editors accept it.

[40] *Ibid.*, X, 336.

[41] He must have known of Giles Fletcher's experience, who offered thanks to God that he had escaped from the worst tyrant in history. Fuller tells the story—evidently on good authority—that Fletcher expressed "his thankfulness to God for his safe return from so great a danger; for the poets cannot fansie Ulysses more glad to be come out of the den of Polyphemus than he was to be rid out of the power of such a barbarous Prince." See *Russia at the Close of the Sixteenth Century*, p. cxxiii.

of course overlaid with centuries of association.[42] But
though long before Milton's time the identification with the
Canaries had been made, no such rationalization is to be
found in the lines of *Paradise Lost*. It is the same with
Aetna. The classics had immortalized Aetna as the Volcano
and as the site of Hell-mouth; and the mountain continued
to hold that reputation in spite of everything Hakluyt and
Arngrimus Jonas—the latter unwillingly—did to dislodge
it in favor of Hecla in Iceland. It is true that Aetna had
been active in the sixteenth and seventeenth centuries; but
there is a classical flavor about Milton's allusions which
leaves little doubt that he was thinking of older times.
When, for instance, he describes the soil in hell where
Satan's feet came to rest, he chooses the following comparison:

> As when the force
> Of subterranean wind transports a Hill
> Torn from *Pelorus*, or the shatter'd side
> Of thundring *Aetna*, whose combustible
> And fewel'd entrals thence conceiving Fire,
> Sublim'd with Mineral fury, aid the Winds,
> And leave a singed bottom all involv'd
> With stench and smoak: Such resting found the sole
> Of unblest feet (Bk. i, ll. 230-238).[42a]

Moreover, the reference of *In Quintum Novembris* is, if
anything, more classical yet:

> Qualia Trinacria trux ab Jove clausus in Aetna
> Efflat tabifico monstrosus ab ore Tiphoeus (ll. 36-37).

We can speculate as to why the poet chose to emphasize
Aetna rather than, say, Vesuvius. He had actually beheld
the latter, which had erupted again only seven years before
his visit to Naples. But perhaps just that difference in his
experience was one factor in making him prefer Aetna. In
Prolusions[43] he recommends that his reader "approach un-

---

[42] See R. R. Cawley, *Unpathed Waters*, pp. 3-15.

[42a] Miss Nicolson (*University of Toronto Quarterly*, vii, 500-513) makes
a case for Milton's having added his experience.

[43] *Works*, xii, 171. Later, also in the *Prolusions* (xii, 229), he wrote,
"Neither Aetna nor Avernus emits anything more noisome."

harmed flame-capped Aetna." Thus construed, his frequent mention may be due partly, as has been suggested,[44] to a kind of suppressed desire, his nobler impulses having thwarted his moving on into Sicily. One further consideration is that the overwhelming number of references in drama favor Aetna rather than Vesuvius.[45] In all, the reader comes away with the conviction that the real determining factor was the classics, which had left their indelible impression.

There is plenty of substantiating evidence to prove that this was apt to be Milton's approach. The phrase "ruddy waves," of Psalm 136,[46] implies perhaps belief in the actual color of the water, whereas travelers had exposed it for the superstition it was.[47] With the pigmies[48] it would naturally have been out of keeping to mention their African counterparts. Similarly Syrtis[49] would call forth no analogy with the notorious Goodwin sands so dreaded by all who sailed the English coast. The peninsula would remain "Chersonese"[50] in spite of Heylyn's writing[51] "*Aurea Chersonesus in India*, which we now call *Malaca*." Ophiusa,[52] Tarsus,[53] and Syene[54] would preserve their original forms for the same reason.

Other cases exist where there is definite evidence dis-

[44] See Gilbert, *op.cit.*, p. 11.

[45] See Sugden's *Topographical Dict.*, p. 5.

[46] L. 45.

[47] How seriously the whole matter was taken may be seen in what Sir Thomas Browne writes. See his chapter "Of the Red Sea" in *Pseudodoxia*, *Works* (Wilkin ed.), III, 259-262. See also R. R. Cawley, "Sir Thomas Browne and His Reading," PMLA, XLVIII (1933), 444-446.

[48] *P.L.*, Bk. I, ll. 780-781.

[49] *P.L.*, Bk. II, ll. 939-940.

[50] *P.L.*, Bk. XI, l. 392. Cf. also *P.R.*, Bk. IV, l. 74.

[51] *Cosmographie*, II, 121.

[52] *P.L.*, Bk. X, ll. 526-528. As Verity says, Ovid and Lucan underlie the passage.

[53] *S.A.*, l. 715. Josephus had made the identification of Tarshish with Tarsus, according to Gilbert (*op.cit.*, p. 285), but a later authority, Bochart, had denied it.

[54] *P.R.*, Bk. IV, l. 70. Syene is "farthest South" because Pliny had spoken of it as one limit of the Roman Empire. The modern name is Assouan. See Gilbert, *op.cit.*, p. 282.

proving what Milton says or implies. There is, however, justification in the considerable doubt he shows about the exact site of Ur.[55] Gilbert[56] has pointed out how he appears to have moved it about. "From the reference to Haran," said Verity,[57] "we may conjecture that M. supposed Ur to be in Upper Mesopotamia, i.e. at least 400 miles north of its real site." The confusion seems to have arisen, not merely in Milton's mind but in the minds of most others, because the "Chaldaeans" ranged over quite a little territory. What many identified as Ur was actually far south of Chaldaea strictly so called; but the tribe, who appear to have had nomadic inclinations, penetrated southwards. Heylyn,[58] who could have been resorted to as a competent authority on the subject, wrote that Ur of the Chaldees got its name, "either because the Chaldees were in those daies possessed of the place; or because the name of Chaldaea did comprehend also those parts of this Countrey which lay towards Tigris, as was shewn before. For that the place from which Terah the Father of Abraham did return to Haran in Mesopotamia, was rather situate in this coast where Ur is placed by Ammianus, than betwixt the Lakes of Chaldaea and the Persian Golf, where most Writers place it, may appear probable for these reasons." And he goes on to give sufficient basis for his conclusion. Actually the problem is less complicated than some of the editors have made it. Milton's *"Ur of Chaldaea"* is, after all, only a slight remove from the Biblical "Ur of the Chaldees," and the authority of the Bible[59] was all he needed.

When we move down into the later periods, we find Milton still inclined to follow the traditional. This is true, for instance, in his mention of Mecca. It occurs in a passage of *Eikonoklastes*[60] which is obviously figurative and in

---

[55] *P.L.*, Bk. xii, l. 130.
[57] *Paradise Lost*, p. 645.
[59] See Genesis 11:31.

[56] *Op.cit.*, pp. 306-307.
[58] *Cosmographie*, iii, 135.
[60] *Works*, v, 169-170.

which he is half paraphrasing his opponent; he says there that the comparison's appropriateness can be judged by those, "who have travell'd to *Mecca*, That the Parlament have hung the majestie of Kingship in an airy imagination of regality between the Privileges of both Houses, like the Tombe of Mahomet." About this there was a perfect conspiracy of error, and there was error of two kinds firmly refuted by later travelers. Marlowe[61] was only one of many to place the tomb at Mecca rather than Medina. Evelyn[62] himself makes the mistake. But Sandys[63] and Purchas[64] enter categorical denials. The former, describing Medina, wrote, "that [tomb] of Mahomet (not hanging in the aire as reported) is covered with greene." And similarly Purchas, also describing Medina, declared that the tomb was "not in an iron Chest attracted by Adamant at Mecca, as some affirme." Whatever travelers Milton might have known at first hand, it is clear he knew Purchas and Sandys, though he chose in such instances to disregard their evidence.

With Ormus, an island city in the Persian Gulf, the story is somewhat the same. It had been one of the most important trading centers and had been brought vividly to Englishmen's attention by Newbery's letter.[65] Hakluyt[66] referred to Ormus as the "most famous Mart towne of all East India, whither all ye merchandises of India are brought." Heylyn[67]

---

[61] See R. R. Cawley, *Voyagers and Elizabethan Drama*, p. 178.

[62] See Gilbert, *op.cit.*, p. 248.

[63] *Relation* (1621), p. 125.

[64] *Pilgrimage* (1613), p. 226.

Gilbert (*op.cit.*, p. 185) quotes Varthema: "Opportunitie now serveth to confute the opinion of them which thinke that the Arke or Tombe of wicked Mahumet in Mecha to hang in the Ayre, not borne up with any thing. I . . . saw the place where Mahumet is buried, in the said Citie of Medina." Later in life, it was especially that kind of eye-witness evidence that appealed to Milton.

[65] See Hakluyt, *op.cit.*, v, 457. The whole matter, of some importance, may be read in Foster's *England's Quest of Eastern Trade*, p. 94. See also an article "Ormuz and Amurath," TLS, March 30, 1933.

[66] *Op.cit.*, III, 147.   [67] *Microcosmos* (1636), p. 635.

similarly plays up the city's commercial importance: "Ormus . . . much famed, for that it standeth conveniently for
the trafficke of India, Persia, and Arabia." And he goes into
considerable detail about its vast wealth. Possibly an even
more determining factor was the existence of a proverb
which, proverb-like, tended to set an impression in people's
minds. It is what one most often reads about Ormus;
Verity[68] quotes Coryat's version, who praises Venice, "of
which the inhabitants may as proudly vaunt as I have read
the Persians have done of their Ormus, who say that if the
world were a ring, then should Ormus be the gem thereof."
In light of these two circumstances Professor Draper[69] was
perhaps unduly concerned that Milton should have chosen
Ormus as a symbol of luxury long after it had lapsed into
obscurity following the Persian-British capture in 1622:

> High on a Throne of Royal State, which far
> Outshon the wealth of *Ormus* and of *Ind*
> . . . .
> Satan exalted sat (Bk. ii, ll. 1-5).

The answer is to be found, partly at least, in the proverb
from Mandelslo which Draper quotes.[70]

Few reputations were more firmly established than that
of Mount Tenerife in the Canaries. Here the travelers were
as much at fault as the literary fellows for they seemed to
vie with one another to see who could indulge in the most
extravagant hyperbole. Heylyn,[71] who is often moderate, is
one of the most guilty in this instance: "Tenariffe . . . is
most remarkable for a Mountain of so great an height,
that it may be seen 90 Leagues at Sea, in a fair clear day.
Some reckon it 15 miles high, others 15. Leagues, and some
advance it to 60 miles, but with little credit. With truth
enough most of our Travellers and Geographers hold it to

[68] *Op.cit.*, p. 400.
[69] "Milton's Ormus," MLR, xx (1925), 323-327.
[70] Heylyn also carries the proverb. See *Cosmographie*, iii, 167.
[71] *Cosmographie*, iv, 88.

be the highest in the whole world." The last estimate would make it a mere ten times higher than Everest. If anything like this was an Englishman's conception of the mountain,[72] Milton's comparison must have acquired particular impressiveness:

> On th' other side *Satan* allarm'd
> Collecting all his might dilated stood,
> Like *Teneriff* or *Atlas* unremov'd (Bk IV, ll. 985-987).

With the mention[73] of the Sultan "Turchestan-born" we again observe the poet's deliberately following an older tradition. Heylyn[74] had cast some doubt on the theory of the Turks' having come originally from Turchestan: "That their whole body setled here [Turchestan], and from hence made their conquest of *Persia*, as some very industrious men are of opinion, I by no means grant. . . . So that it is not to be doubted but that they came first into *Persia* out of *Turcomania*, and not out of *Turchestan*." But the very fact that he labors the point proves how current the theory was.

A superstition even more widespread than Tenerife was the one which connected Lapland with witches. Nobody knows how the theory originated,[75] but it has been conjectured that the Laplanders themselves encouraged the reputation in order to keep unwanted visitors from their shores. However that may be, the tradition was so strong in Milton's time that "Laplander" was intelligible as a witch or sorcerer.[76] Among travelers there had been plenty of authority. Not merely had that great favorite Richard Eden[77] vouched for the fact but, as we have seen,[78] Giles Fletcher Sr.,[79] than whom there was no better authority of

---

[72] For the commonness of the ascription, see R. R. Cawley, *Voyagers and Elizabethan Drama*, pp. 98-99.

[73] *P.L.*, Bk. XI, ll. 395-396.　　　　[74] *Cosmographie*, III, 196.

[75] It goes back at least to Snorri.

[76] See Cavendish's *Variety* (*Two Comedies*, 1649), p. 4.

[77] *Notes Upon Russia*, II, 225.　　　　[78] See p. 50 *supra*.

[79] Hakluyt, *op.cit.*, III, 404.

the time, had written: "For practise of witchcraft and sorcerie they [the Lapps] passe all nations in the worlde." Such a story provided the dramatists with a picturesque figure, and they made full use of it.[80] In fact, one meets the ascription so often that he finds it almost surprising that Milton should place witches and sorcerers anywhere else. *In Quintum Novembris*[81] carries an allusion to Etrurian sorcerers. And in *Prolusions*[82] Milton asks, "has some Thessalian witch smeared me with magic ointment?" Research in such authorities as Fletcher and Heylyn taught him better. The latter[83] wrote of a part of Lapland that they had nights three months long, "during which time lurking in their Caves, they have leisure to consult with the *Prince of Darknesse.*" And he goes on to tell how they are sorcerers, recounting the familiar story of their raising winds and tempests. By the time of *A Brief History of Moscovia* Milton[84] writes as one having authority when he speaks familiarly of the "Witches of the *Samoeds, Lappians* and *Tartarians.*" *Paradise Lost* is therefore "up-to-date" when the Night-Hag is described as riding through the air,

> to dance
> With *Lapland* Witches (Bk. ii, ll. 664-665).

Of far older origin was the tradition that the River Nile had seven mouths. Milton recognizes this convention when he has Michael explaining to Adam the world's future events and describing,

> *Egypt*, divided by the River *Nile*;
> See where it flows, disgorging at seaven mouthes
> Into the Sea (Bk. xii, ll. 157-159).[85]

Not many years before, Sir Thomas Browne had spent a good part of one chapter of *Pseudodoxia Epidemica* proving

---

[80] See Sugden, *op.cit.*, p. 299. Also R. R. Cawley, *op.cit.*, pp. 250-252.
[81] L. 51.   [82] *Works*, xii, 241.
[83] *Cosmographie*, ii, 156.   [84] *Works*, x, 361.
[85] See similar use in *Prolusions, Works*, xii, 325.

that the Nile could not possibly have seven mouths, any way you wished to figure it.[86] But Virgil and Ovid were formidable obstacles to surmount, and Fuller[87] still talked glibly of the seven mouths. With the dramatists the number is virtually stereotyped.[88] The other part of Milton's passage, on the contrary, shows a tendency to use the new geography. The older maps had represented Egypt as having Nilus for its eastern boundary. But the maps for a hundred years before *Paradise Lost*, Ortelius, Mercator, Purchas, had shown the country as divided.[89] The last-named[90] had written explicitly: "Nilus runneth through the middest thereof."

Besides the number of mouths, one of the most common associations with the Nile was the mud which spawned monsters by interaction with the sun. Spenser's famous simile[91] which has forever imprinted the dragon Error on our minds, the one in which he says that the Nile's "fattie waves doe fertile slime outwell," is only one of almost countless references to this phenomenon.[92] In fact, both the travel-literature and literature itself so swarm with such allusions that one feels that Milton, son of Spenser as he was, must have exercised some restraint when he was describing Satan returned to Pandemonium:

> Now Dragon grown, larger then whom the Sun
> Ingenderd in the *Pythian* Vale on slime,
> Huge *Python* (Bk. x, ll. 529-531).

The passage is Ovidian and nothing but Ovid.[93]

[86] For fuller discussion cf. R. R. Cawley, *Voyagers and Elizabethan Drama*, pp. 39-40. Also "Sir Thomas Browne and His Reading," PMLA, XLVIII (1933), 458-462.

[87] Gilbert, *op.cit.*, p. 208. But in *Pisgah-Sight* (Book IV, 82) Fuller makes an impressive list of those who disagree with the traditional number.

[88] See Sugden, *op.cit.*, p. 367 and R. R. Cawley, *op.cit.*, p. 40.

[89] See R. R. Cawley, *op.cit.*, p. 11.

[90] *Pilgrimage* (1613), p. 469.   [91] *F.Q.*, I, i, 21.

[92] See R. R. Cawley, *op.cit.*, p. 46ff. and Sugden, *op.cit.*, p. 367.

[93] See C. G. Osgood, *Classical Mythology of Milton's English Poems*, p. 71.

It is hoped, for one thing, that the foregoing discussion as indicating on Milton's part a general attitude towards his material may throw some light on such a passage as the one where the poet carefully distinguishes between Cambalu and Pekin, between Cathay and China.[94] It will be recalled that Michael unfolds to Adam the various regions of the world:

> from the destind Walls
> Of *Cambalu*, seat of *Cathaian Can*
> . . . .
> To *Paquin* of *Sinaean* Kings (Bk. xi, ll. 387-390).

Long beyond the time when he was intellectually convinced of the contrary, Milton would go on using conceptions merely for their poetic effect. Clearly the passage is far richer for the double associations with fabled Cambalu and its attendant Khan, with swarming Pekin and the boundless regions ruled over by Chinese kings.

[94] Cf. discussion of these lines pp. 12-13 *supra*.

CHAPTER V

A GROWING CONSCIENCE

THERE comes now a kind of middle period in the growth of Milton's knowledge. It is not taking too much liberty to say that he was progressively developing a geographic conscience. Though it may seem like a contradiction, this period actually represented in him a liberalizing tendency which kept step with the development of his mind in other ways. There were various reasons for this. The tutoring he did from 1640 must have contributed its share. If he was to teach the Phillips brothers, he would wish to know what was the latest on any subject. Davity's *Estates, Empires, and Principallities of the World*[1] may not have suited his own taste at the time, but it would at least have afforded him much information that was reasonably current. A far more important contributing factor, however, was the official position which came nearly a decade later. One has only to think what that meant to Milton. What he may have learned about European governments is, except for Russia, not our concern here. But the correspondence over which he had either direct or indirect supervision immeasurably broadened his knowledge of foreign lands beyond the European horizon.[2] Through it possessions in the far west as well as the far east became better known to him. A man in such a position could not have helped learning much about the activities of the great East India Company,[3] for instance, whose long fingers

---

[1] *Les Empires, Royaumes, Estats, et Principautez du Monde*, Paris, 1614. Translated in 1615. See A. H. Gilbert, "Pierre Davity: His Geography and its Use by Milton," *Geog. Rev.*, VII (1919), 322-336.

[2] One paper, for instance, speaks of what was "lost of the fruits in the *Molucca* Islands, *Banda* and *Amboyna*, from the time that by the slaughter of our men we were thence expell'd" (see *Works*, XIII, 135).

[3] For possible influence of the Company, see an article, "Ormuz and Amurath," TLS, March 30, 1933.

reached so far around the globe. And through that Company he would become progressively aware of the vital importance of trade all over the world, especially since this was a period when England's commerce was expanding so rapidly in some quarters. This in turn would tend to make him conversant with distant nations and climes.[4] It is an ever-widening circle.

Another factor of prime significance is the research Milton was doing in this middle period for his *Brief History of Moscovia*. A somewhat earlier date for the work than has been assigned by several scholars appears probable.[5] It seems likely that it may have been composed in part while he still had in mind textbooks for his pupils. However that may be, it is obvious that in the 1640 decade he was learning much about that strange, barbarous, yet in some ways civilized, country of Russia. In his thoroughgoing way he read the best authorities he could lay his hands on, Fletcher and Hakluyt and Purchas. One thing that emerges clearly from the finished work is his increasing insistence on the eyewitness account. The upshot of his Preface is that so far as possible he will depend on those who have actually seen —Hakluyt appealed to him because he regularly went to firsthand sources; the interesting list at the end has titles which point in the same direction; and while he is investigating "the eastern Bounds of *Russia*, to the Walls of *Cathay*" he seizes almost avidly on the evidence furnished by the Russian travelers "who describe the Countreys in their way far otherwise than our common Geographers."[6] Thus construed, the little *History* becomes a kind of step-

---

[4] He had a hand in a considerable number of letters protesting the abuse of English seamen by foreign powers in remote regions such as Amboyna. "Neither is it pleasant to remember that cruel and bloody Business of Amboyna towards the English, for which no Satisfaction at all hath been given, though often demanded." *Works*, XVIII, 13.

[5] I am in substantial agreement with the arguments set forth by J. A. Bryant, Jr., "Milton and the Art of History," PQ, XXIX (1950), 15-30.

[6] *Works*, X, 328.

pingstone between the earlier poetry and the later. Because he had investigated Russia, he was able to point up certain passages in *Paradise Lost* through mention of specific and connotative names.[7] The terrible description of Sin and Death making their horrid way towards earth takes on pungency when they are compared to two Polar Winds which drive Mountains of Ice,

> that stop th' imagin'd way
> Beyond *Petsora* Eastward (Bk. x, ll. 291-292).

Of Pechora he had read in Purchas,[8] and of how the regions beyond are stopped up to the northeast "with such huge Mountaines of Ice." He gives it some prominence in the *History*, and on the river of like name he speaks of "certain Merchants of Hull" as wintering in 1611. These unfortunates can readily be identified from source.[9] The incident had clearly impressed the region on Englishmen's minds, and Milton was not slow to sense the telling effect of such an allusion.

Naturally such research as he was conducting opened his eyes also to a vast body of peripheral literature. Here we have the evidence of the Commonplace Book. He refers to matters in Purchas well beyond the borders of Russia. The Indians in Sumatra, he notes,[10] are great gluttons, who "renew thire stomack by chewing an hearb called Arecca betula." And his authority as he gives it is "Purchas tom 1.132." On the subject of Numidian poets he refers[11] to "Leo Afer edit Lugdun. 1.2.212." All this reading did not really affect his essential nationalism, as has sometimes been argued. He quotes[12] Speed (Sto. p. 94) with obvious approval: "[It is] a dangerous thing, and an ominous thing,

---

[7] See article by L. C. Tihany, "Milton's 'Brief History of Moscovia,'" *Philol. Quart.*, XIII (1934), 305-306. See also Verity, *op.cit.*, pp. 595-596 *et passim*.

[8] *Pilgrimes*, XIII, 187.

[9] Cf. p. 58 *supra*.

[10] *Works*, XVIII, 132.

[11] *Works*, XVIII, 139.

[12] *Works*, XVIII, 168.

to imitate with earnestnesse the fashions of neighbour nations. so the english ran madding after the French in Edward confessors time. god turn the omen from these days." And probably without being particularly aware that he was entering a very active controversy of his day, he wrote deploringly:

Here Pilgrims roam, that stray'd so farr to seek
In *Golgotha* him dead, who lives in Heav'n (Bk. III, ll. 476-477).

On the other extreme, there are those that argue for a period of "nationalism" and in part misinterpret the very work under consideration. *A Brief History* without doubt proves Milton's admiration for his native land. It can be read also as showing his very real interest in and, up to a point, admiration for foreign lands. For present purposes, then, it represents a widening rather than a narrowing of his vision.

It is observable that this widening did not immediately show itself in his literary works. With few exceptions the prose works of this middle period might have been written by a man whose concern with other countries of his time was superficial. This may strike us as inexplicable until we consider the nature of those prose tracts. A scholar-opponent like Salmasius would naturally argue in classical and Biblical examples. It would be just as natural that Milton should answer him with instances drawn from the ancients and the Bible.[13] Similarly, few voyaging allusions occur in a *History of Britain*.[14] But the *History of Britain*, it will be remembered, stops with the Conquest. Certainly one could hardly expect to find such allusions in a Treatise

[13] On the other hand, when he is matching his wits against Bishop Hall, he is capable of bandying some of the travel terms purveyed in *Mundus Alter et Idem*. Cf. *Apology*, esp. *Works*, III, 294, 300 and *Animadversions*, *Works*, III, 138.

[14] There are a reasonable number of voyaging figures. But certainly no more than the average Englishman would have used in a work of such length.

on Christian Doctrine, or in a work on Logic. A considerable body of the prose thus automatically excludes itself. In the rest there are occasional references such as the one in *Areopagitica*, where he speaks[15] of the Indian voyage "sail'd either by the North of *Cataio* Eastward, or of *Canada* Westward." But, on the whole, fewer than one might expect. We might expect also that he would turn his back on the "long Stories of absurd Superstitions" which he decries in the *Brief History*. And that is just what we find him doing. Even in *Prolusions*[16] he refers jestively to being dubbed "Father," a prodigy, "surpassing the strange tales of Pliny." This does not mean of course that he did not continue to make use of those same "absurd Superstitions" where he found them poetically expedient. It does mean that he reduced their number. And the new travel books he was reading at this period were to a large extent responsible for that reduction.

Among such books it is not difficult to isolate his favorites. Heylyn was obviously one of them. The popularity of his *Cosmographie* is shown by the fact, already mentioned, that there were issues in 1652, 1657, 1660, 1665, 1666, and 1670.[17] Heylyn's ideal of Geography,[18] "without some knowledge wherein, the study of History is neither so pleasant, nor so profitable, as a judicious Reader would desire to have it," parallels Milton's own,[19] "the study of Geography is both profitable and delightfull." Furthermore, in these broader issues it is quite likely that Heylyn helped, with Giles Fletcher, to determine Milton's attitude towards Russia, for his book contained some of the worst arraign-

---

[15] *Works*, IV, 313. [16] *Works*, XII, 241.

[17] CBEL, I, 766. Heylyn's earlier publication was called *Microcosmos, Or a Little Description of the Great World. A Treatise Historicall, Geographicall, Politicall, Theologicall.* Of it there were issues in 1621, 1625, 1627, 1629, 1633, 1636, and 1639.

[18] *Op.cit.*, "Generall Introduction," p. 20.

[19] See Preface to *A Brief History*.

ments of the Muscovites.[20] Generally speaking, it may be said that Milton looked upon him as an authority since he was willing to follow him perhaps more closely than any other traveler. The long passages from *Paradise Lost* and *Regained* discussed in previous chapters seem to give sufficient evidence to prove how far he was willing to accept the geographic details afforded by Heylyn.

But there is considerable other evidence. At times it goes so far as to be determinative in choosing him rather than a different source which has more regularly been cited. The lines on Amara treated above[21] are a case in point. Other travelers give some of the details. Heylyn alone gives, in brief compass, what Milton has, the Mountain itself, the fact that some consider it the Earthly Paradise, that it is under the Equator, is enclosed with shining Rock, that it is "a whole dayes journey high," and that there "*Abassin* Kings thir issue Guard." To take another example, Milton writes of "*Samarchand* by *Oxus, Temirs* Throne."[22] Tamburlaine was of course a familiar figure. Samarkand was reasonably well known. But Heylyn refers to "*Samarchand,* the Seat Royall of *Tamerlane*" as being "on the North-side of *Oxus*"; and in a century when orthography was, to say the least, unstable spells the city exactly like Milton.[23] Heylyn may even be used to explain his mistake in placing the city "by *Oxus*."[24] Much the same may be said for a passage in Book x where the poet is describing the effects of the fall interfering with the sun,

[20] "The people," wrote Heylyn (*op.cit.,* II, 150), "as it is commonly reported of them, are very perfidious, crafty and deceitful in all their bargains, . . . making no reckoning of their promises, and studying nothing more then wayes to evade their Contracts."

[21] Cf. pp. 69-70 *supra.*

[22] Cf. p. 12 *supra.*

[23] Purchas, whom Gilbert (*op.cit.,* pp. 252-253) quotes, spells "Samercand" (or "Samarcand"), and makes no mention of Oxus. The passage is discussed by Whiting, *op.cit.,* p. 120.

[24] See p. 12 note 8 *supra.*

which had forbid the Snow
From cold *Estotiland*, and South as farr
Beneath *Magellan* (Bk. x, ll. 685-687).

In an important section immediately following his short general section on America, Heylyn[25] writes "Of Estotiland" (in very large letters) and says, "first *Estotiland* specially so called, is the most Northern Region on the East side of *America*." This gives Milton his extreme northern limit which he needed for the passage in question. Three lines below, Heylyn refers to "the extream cold of the Country." Furthermore, on his general map of America[26] he similarly spells the region "Estotiland."[27] Only four pages later,[28] in the next section, "Of Canada," he has "Norumbega" in large letters, and Milton is to speak within ten lines "of *Norumbega*."

One more example may be taken, from a passage which has been in controversy. Satan has just alighted on the convex of this world's firm opacous Globe and is compared to a vulture "on *Imaus* bred" which,

flies toward the Springs
Of *Ganges* or *Hydaspes*, *Indian* streams (Bk. iii, ll. 435-436).

In his discussion of these lines Professor Whiting[29] notes that "this river [Hydaspis] is very rarely named on contemporary maps." But Heylyn[30] happens to be one who gives a prominent position to the river, speaking of "the famous Rivers *Indus, Hidaspis* . . . [which] have their first beginnings. In this point do they [Taurus Mts.] hold their heads exceeding high, to equal the Mountains of *Imaus*." Later[31] Heylyn mentions "Hydaspes," spelled precisely like Milton,

---

[25] *Op.cit.* (1652), Bk. iv, 103. Gilbert (*op.cit.*, pp. 117-118) quotes Hakluyt.

[26] See *op.cit.*, map preceding page 95.

[27] Isaac Taylor (*Notes and Queries*, Ser. viii, No. vii, pp. 421, 461-462) is at some pains to proclaim that he has found "Estotilande" on a Paris map of 1694 by a certain H. A. Jaillot.

[28] P. 107.   [29] *Op.cit.*, pp. 117-118.

[30] *Op.cit.*, iii, 140.   [31] *Op.cit.*, iii, 216.

first: "Principall Rivers of this part, 1 *Hydaspes*." And two pages beyond[32] he mentions the river twice, with the same spelling. As for the much disputed "Sericana," Heylyn,[33] like Ortelius, mentions "Serica" (once more in large letters) only a few pages before. It is further possible that the close connection Milton draws between Sericana and the Chinese may have been suggested by Heylyn,[34] who mentions "*Cambalu*, supposed to be the *Issedan Serica* of the Antients, and like enough to be that City of the *Cathayans*, which made that notable resistance unto *Cingis*." Just below he again refers to Serica and almost at once to "the mountains of *Imaus*." It might be noted in passing that he carries, some ten pages later, the story of the Chinese "*Carts* and *Coaches*" which are "driven with *sayles*." But not too much should be made of this since few contemporary accounts of China appeared without some mention of the famous sail-wagons.[35]

Occasionally spelling is determinative. Verity[36] called attention to the fact that the forms "Rhene" and "Danaw" which Milton[37] used are to be found in both Hexham and Heylyn. A spelling like "Almansor," on the other hand, is so exceptional that the poet's use of it[38] may well prove its provenience in Heylyn since that traveler spells it exactly the same way.

[32] P. 218. [33] *Op.cit.*, III, 199.
[34] *Op.cit.* (1670), pp. 854-855. [35] Cf. *P.L.*, Bk. III, ll. 437-439.
Gilbert (*op.cit.*, p. 263) refers to Mendoza, Bertius, Davity, Ortelius, and Mercator. A Speed map of China (1626) contains the same legend. Escalante and B. Jonson also allude to the custom. See R. R. Cawley, *Voyagers and Elizabethan Drama*, pp. 225-226 and notes.
[36] *Paradise Lost*, p. 382. [37] *P.L.*, Bk. I, l. 353.
[38] See pp. 17-18 *supra*.
Purchas is one of the very few who so spell it. "The golden *Chersonese*" of Bk. XI, l. 392 (see discussion p. 14 *supra*) is another case in point since Heylyn has Milton's exact spelling four times (in fact, it is his usual spelling), and twice has "the Golden Chersonese." See *op.cit.*, III, 187 (bis), 241, and 254. To show how fluid orthography was, Milton himself spells "Chersoness" the next time (*P.R.*, Bk. IV, l. 74). For many other instances where Milton has followed Heylyn's spelling, see Chapters I and II *supra*.

Another way in which Milton may have employed the cosmographer is in making him stand sponsor for certain doubtful allusions. We have seen[39] how geographers' exaggerations were responsible for giving poetry an apt figure of extreme height. Thus when Milton is at special pains to create the impression of Satan's overwhelming stature as he fronts Gabriel's armed guard, he can think of no better comparison than Tenerife unremoved. If he needed any authority, Heylyn himself gave him ample by recording that some estimated the mountain at fifteen miles, others at fifteen leagues. We have seen[40] also how the poet did not hesitate to use Ormus as a symbol of splendor and wealth long after the city had fallen into decay. Here once more if he was looking for support, he might have found it in Heylyn,[41] who wrote of "Ormus, not so much memorable for the greatness, as the wealth"; and who went on to say that it became so rich that the Kings' tributes from it "amounted to 14000 Seriffs yearly." Some scholars have debated over why Milton appears to make "Hesperides" a place rather than people. In *Paradise Regained*[42] he refers to "Ladies of th' *Hesperides*." But for this too there was ample authority in Heylyn,[43] who wrote: "The daughters of this Atlas dwelt in the Ilands Hesperides, situate in the Atlanticke Ocean." And later[44] he said: "The Hesperides by Pliny and Pomponius Mela . . . are said to be two in number, situate in the Atlantick Seas . . . habitation to the daughters of Atlas (which they call by the name of Hesperides also)."

But it was not like Milton to accept any book as a final authority, and he does not hesitate to differ with Heylyn whenever it suits his purpose. Characteristically he reserved judgment. The cosmographer may argue at some length

[39] See p. 80 *supra*.
[41] *Op.cit.*, III, 167.
[43] *Microcosmos*, p. 715.
[40] See pp. 78-79 *supra*.
[42] Bk. II, l. 357.
[44] *Op.cit.*, p. 1007. In the *Cosmographie* the reference is at Bk. IV, 90.

against deriving the Turks from Turchestan;[45] in *Paradise Lost* the Sultan is still "*Turchestan*-born." Heylyn[46] can show unequivocally that Ur is not, strictly speaking, in Chaldaea; yet Milton can refer without hesitation to "*Ur of Chaldaea*." Here undoubtedly a well-known Biblical expression was decisive. The *Cosmographie* carefully identifies Tremisen with Algiers;[47] whereas the poet seems to distinguish them. Finally, Milton[48] goes counter to Heylyn's explicit placing of "the Aethiopian Ocean" when he moves it over to the east of Africa and makes his intrepid sailors ply stemming nightly towards the Pole; though in this instance his blindness might have played its determining role.

On the other hand, we can safely conclude that Milton was not merely familiar with the *Cosmographie* but that he was willing to take it as a considerable authority and to resort to it when there came a question of geographic accuracy. Indeed, it may even be used, somewhat as we use North's *Plutarch* with Shakespeare, to explain certain passages which are otherwise not altogether explicable. For example, the poet has somehow managed to confuse Ecbatan with modern Tabriz or Tauris.[49] But Heylyn before him had made the same confusion. To what extent Milton was willing to follow him in detail has, it is hoped, been sufficiently demonstrated in an examination of the two long passages earlier in this study.

With Henry Hexham's translation of Mercator's Atlas (1636-1638), which Verity[50] is inclined to bracket with Heylyn as "the two most popular geographical works of the time," one gets nowhere near the same feeling of presentness. It is true that it was also popular. But Milton seems

---

[45] See p. 15 note 24 *supra.* Also p. 80 *supra.*
[46] See p. 77 *supra.*   [47] See p. 19 *supra.*
[48] See p. 68 note 13 *supra.*   [49] See pp. 14-15 *supra.*
[50] *Op.cit.*, p. 382.
I will henceforth use "Hexham" in order to distinguish this edition of Mercator from others.

to have resorted to it far less often and to have accepted it as authority in no sense as he did Heylyn. Verity[51] considered that he had proved the poet's use of the Atlas in *Lycidas*. He believed that "Namancos" and *"Bayona's* hold" came from Hexham's map of Galicia.[52] Here Verity may have allowed himself to be intrigued by the fact that the Mercator was published in the very year before the elegy was composed. A. S. Cook[53] came along to show that Namancos at least might well derive from many sources. And Professor Whiting[54] has further questioned the Hexham provenience and demonstrated that other sources, Ortelius included, are on the whole more likely. Such doubt applies to an extraordinary number of cases where Hexham has been cited as possibly underlying some passage in Milton. In many of these instances the other source is the one the poet is more apt to have used. It has been shown above[55] that his "cold *Estotiland"* may well go back to Heylyn, who has just that spelling, who gives the country special prominence, and who calls attention to its cold. Hexham[56] gives it no prominence and he spells it "Estotilandia." The other name linked with it was "Norumbega," which Heylyn printed in large letters, spelled as Milton spelled it; whereas Hexham spells "Norembega" (General Map of America) and "Norembegua" (Map of New England). In the same way Verity[57] finds "Ormus Emporium" on Hexham's Map of Persia; however, Heylyn not merely mentions the place but gives details about its wealth.[58] In connection with the lines where Milton describes Satan's flight to the world and compares him with a vulture, Verity[59] cites Hexham's Map of Tartaria. Here again both Ortelius and Heylyn

---

[51] *Comus and Lycidas*, Cambridge, 1898, pp. 152-153.
[52] This discovery really goes back to Todd.
[53] *Modern Language Review*, II (1907), 124-128.
[54] *Op.cit.*, p. 106.　　　　　　　　[55] See p. 90 *supra*.
[56] *Atlas*, p. 436.　　　　　　　　[57] *Op.cit.*, p. 400.
[58] See p. 92 *supra*.　　　　　　　　[59] *Op.cit.*, pp. 683-684.

fit the circumstances as well.[60] Similarly, Milton's forms "Rhene" and "Danaw" appear in Heylyn as well as Hexham. Again, Verity[61] cites Hexham to place "Aspramont"; but, as Gilbert[62] indicates, the associations are far more apt to be with the romances, with Ariosto, Boiardo, and Pulci. As for "*Ternate* and *Tidore*,"[63] the two little spice islands were important out of all proportion to their size. Hexham[64] does speak of the Moluccas as being famous throughout the world and of these two as being "the principallest." They are, however, commonly mentioned and equally played up, Heylyn[65] for one stressing their great importance.

Another category into which the references to Hexham go is the general kind which proves nothing because the matter in hand amounts to common knowledge. Verity[66] quotes in connection with "the tallest Pine hewn on *Norwegian* hills" a passage from Hexham about Norway's regularly supplying such masts. He quotes[67] "Golfo di *Bengala*" for the poet's "close sailing from *Bengala*"; it would be difficult to find a contemporary geography that did not use that form of the word.[68] The same may be said for "Ethiopian,"[69] which has been shown[70] to be the regular way to characterize the sea *west* of Africa. Verity[71] finds the Cathayan "Can" in Hexham, but himself quotes and cites various other passages where the term can be found. Memphis, he points out,[72] was identified by Hexham with Cairo or Alcairo. But that was almost the customary identification.

[60] See p. 90 *supra*.
[61] *Op.cit.*, p. 677.
[62] *Op.cit.*, p. 35.
[63] See *P.L.*, Bk. II, l. 639.
[64] *Atlas*, p. 423.
[65] *Op.cit.*, III, 250.
Purchas and Camões both introduce the islands. For further instances, see R. R. Cawley, *Voyagers and Elizabethan Drama*, pp. 124-125 and note.
[66] *Op.cit.*, p. 379.
[67] *Op.cit.*, p. 417.
[68] Heylyn (*op.cit.*, III, 235), for instance, has "Bengala." Cf. also Hakluyt, *op.cit.*, v, 410; vi, 25; xi, 378; and Purchas' *Pilgrimes*, II, 315; IV, 38; IX, 13.
[69] Verity, *op.cit.*, pp. 417-418.
[70] Cf. pp. 68-69 *supra*.
[71] *Op.cit.*, p. 699.
[72] *Op.cit.*, p. 396.

On the other hand, Verity[73] quotes to explain Milton's catalogue of wind-names,

> *Notus* and *Afer* black with thundrous Clouds
> From *Serraliona* (Bk. x, ll. 702-703),

an apt passage from Hexham: "Sierra Liona is . . . a very high Mount, the toppe whereof is continually hidden with snowe: from whence there comes fearefull noises, and great tempests."

The evidence of spelling likewise comes to bear here. It is true that Hexham carries Milton's spelling of "Atabalipa";[74] but so does Purchas in *Pilgrimes*, which it is known the poet used. Similarly he has "Cusco"; so does Heylyn. With many other spellings there is divergence. Hexham's form is "Motecumo"[75] (for Milton's "Motezume"), "Samarcanda"[76] (for "Samarchand"), "Hydaspis"[77] (for "Hydaspes"), and "Candahar"[78] (for "Candaor").

One noticeable distinction between Hexham and Heylyn is that the former lacks the other's philosophic approach to his material. Hexham often quotes Heylyn as authority,[79] but usually fails to impart his broader preconceptions. Furthermore, Hexham omits the background material in history which Heylyn so customarily introduces into his *Cosmographie*. For example, the former makes no mention of "Salmanassar" and his association with Nineveh.[80] Milton found much use for such historical and pseudo-historical materials. In many instances they enriched his poetry by furnishing the overtones.

With Samuel Purchas we find Milton regarding a traveler in still a third way. There exists the incontrovertible evi-

[73] *Op.cit.*, p. 609.   [74] See p. 20 *supra*.   [75] *Op.cit.*, p. 443.
[76] *Op.cit.*, p. 414.   [77] *Op.cit.*, p. 419.   [78] *Op.cit.*, p. 412.
[79] The *Microcosmos*, of course.
[80] See p. 28 *supra*.
Professor Whiting (*op.cit.*, pp. 23-25) shows that Milton may have borrowed something from Hexham's introductory pages on the subject of Creation.

dence of the Commonplace Book[81] and the table at the end of *Moscovia* that he was familiar with Purchas' work. But except for the *Brief History*, where he would naturally find the *Pilgrimes* very much to his purpose, Milton did not use the material nearly so consecutively as he was willing to use, say, Heylyn. Purchas' huge volumes were rather a storehouse of information from which he might cull an incidental detail here and there. Gilbert[82] argues well that Purchas pleased him better than Davity because the former was more detailed and gave more of an eyewitness account. But this applies rather to the period before he went blind. After darkness came upon him, there is evidence that he preferred the more compendious books. A limit would naturally be set on the amount of reading aloud the amanuenses could do, and what Milton remembers is perhaps the striking individual detail which the leisurely Purchas had impressed on his mind. The traces of *Pilgrimes* we find in *Paradise Lost* are apt, as a matter of fact, to be of that sort. What was said of Hexham may almost equally be said of Purchas, that several passages which appear to owe something to him may just as probably owe that something to one of the other travelers.

The *locus classicus* is the famous Amara passage. It has been customary for scholars to quote Purchas,[83] who has an account that reminds us in many respects of Milton's. But, as has been shown in an earlier chapter,[84] Heylyn is even closer. Much the same may be said for Sofala and its identification with Ophir.[85] Once more, scholars are apt to quote the *Pilgrimes*.[86] Purchas, however, makes no specific mention of Ophir whereas Heylyn[87] writes: "This Country [Sofala] for its abundance of *Gold* and *Ivory*, is by some

[81] *Works*, XVIII, 132, 139.   [82] *Geog. Rev.*, VII, 335.
[83] Cf. Todd's note; also Gilbert (*Geog. Dict.*, pp. 18-20); McColley, *Paradise Lost*, p. 157.
[84] Cf. pp. 69-70 *supra*.   [85] See pp. 15-16 *supra*.
[86] Cf. Gilbert, *op.cit.*, p. 272.   [87] *Cosmographie*, IV, 75.

thought to be that land of *Ophir*, to which *Solomon* sent." Ortelius seems to be an equally good source since it was well known at the time that he was one of those chiefly responsible for the identification.[88] There are other cases which seem even more conclusive. In connection with,

Mombaza, and *Quiloa*, and *Melind*,[89]

descriptive passages from Purchas have been quoted.[90] But Heylyn has all three names on a single page and calls attention to them by printing in large letters. This is just as true of "*Agra* and *Lahor*."[91] We meet a far more complicated problem with the lines which describe the fig tree out of which the fallen Adam and Eve were to fashion their clothes:

> There soon they chose
> The Figtree, not that kind for Fruit renown'd,
> But such as at this day to *Indians* known
> In *Malabar* or *Decan* spreds her Armes
> Braunching so broad and long, that in the ground
> The bended Twigs take root, and Daughters grow
> About the Mother Tree, a Pillard shade
> High overarch't, and echoing Walks between;
> There oft the *Indian* Herdsman shunning heate
> Shelters in coole, and tends his pasturing Herds
> At Loopholes cut through thickest shade: Those Leaves
> They gatherd, broad as *Amazonian* Targe,
> And with what skill they had, together sowd,
> To gird thir waste, vain Covering if to hide
> Thir guilt and dreaded shame (Bk. ix, ll. 1100-1114).

The probability is that we have to do here not with the travelers at all, however Linschoten and Purchas may pass before our vision.[92] It is far more likely that Milton is

---

[88] For instance, Heylyn (*op.cit.*, iv, 75) says that "of this opinion *Ortelius* in his *Thesaurus* was the first Author."

[89] Cf. pp. 15-16 *supra*. Cf. Purchas, *op.cit.*, vi, 512-514.

[90] Cf. Gilbert, *op. cit.*   [91] See pp. 13-14 *supra*.

[92] See Gilbert, *op.cit.*, pp. 181-182. In the originals the passages occur in Linschoten's *Discours of Voyages* (London, 1598), pp. 103-104, and in *Pilgrimes* (1625), ii, 1780.

98

recalling mainly two other passages, one from Pliny and the other, as Warton long ago pointed out, from his faithful redactor, Gerard, in the *Herball*.[93]

There are other passages often linked to particular travel books which contain material of such general knowledge that no specific source can be found. For instance, in connection with,

the parting Sun
Beyond the Earths green Cape and verdant Isles
Hesperean sets (Bk. viii, ll. 630-632),

Thompson[94] quotes Purchas. Gilbert,[95] on the other hand, refers to an apt passage in Hakluyt. While for the same passage Whiting[96] gives Ortelius. The very fact that such a multiplicity of "sources" should be cited is perhaps sufficient to prove that there is no source in any strict sense. Actually such a reference is close to being a commonplace of the time.[97] Similarly Gilbert[98] is quite aware, when he quotes *Pilgrimes* for,

Groves whose rich Trees wept odorous Gumms
and Balme (Bk. iv, l. 248),

that he is giving *e pluribus unum*.

It is tempting, on the contrary, to trace certain lines in Milton back to individual passages in Purchas. The Pliny chapter which presumably underlies the "dark *Iberian* dales" of *Paradise Regained*[99] has no suggestion of darkness.[100] Purchas[101] speaks of a "Kingdome of Georgia" a province of which "is all covered over with such thicke and palpable darknesse that none can see anything therein." It should be

---

[93] See Gilbert, *op.cit.*, p. 182, and *The Herball* (London, 1597), pp. 1330-1331.

[94] sp, xvi, 168. [95] *Op.cit.*, p. 133. [96] *Op.cit.*, pp. 99-100.

[97] Milton himself was somewhat given to describing the sun sinking beyond the western isles. Cf. *P.L.*, Bk. iv, ll. 352-354, 591-592.

[98] *Op.cit.*, p. 156. [99] Bk. iii, l. 318.

[100] See *Natural History*, ii, 20.

[101] Quoted by Gilbert, *op.cit.*, p. 151.

noticed, however, that Heylyn,[102] in connection with his "Iberia," which he prints in large letters, says that the country is covered with "woods, and thickets." It is likewise tempting to accept *Pilgrimes* as the authority for Milton's shifting the seat of the Persian monarchy,[103]

> or where
> The *Persian* in *Ecbatan* sate, or since
> In *Hispahan* (Bk. xi, ll. 392-394).

Gilbert[104] quotes appropriately from Purchas:

[Casbeen] is now one of the seats of the Persian Kings Empire, which was translated by King Tamas, this Kings grandfather, from Tauris, . . . though the King that now raigneth makes most of his abode in Hispaan, fourteen daies journey farther towards the East.

If Milton was as careful with spelling as we have good evidence that he was, we are justified also in mentioning Purchas with "Ercoco," the utmost port of Negus' empire.[105] The spelling is certainly not the usual one, though it is to be found in Leo[106] as well as Ortelius. It is the form usually found in *Pilgrimes*.[107] With the,

> Mountains of Ice, that stop th' imagin'd way
> Beyond *Petsora* Eastward (Bk. x, ll. 291-292),

we have the almost incontestable evidence of *A Brief History of Moscovia* to prove that Milton was actually thinking back to the voyages of Gourdon of Hull or of Pet-Jackman, as he had read them in the pages of Purchas.[108] In addition, there were undoubtedly some striking pages which, when read originally, would have made so deep an impression on the poet's mind that he did not need the services of an amanuensis to read them over from so discursive an account

---

[102] *Cosmographie*, iii, 147.   [103] See pp. 14-15 *supra*.
[104] *Op.cit.*, pp. 146-147.
[105] *P.L.*, Bk. xi, ll. 397-398. See p. 16 *supra*.
[106] See p. 16 note 28 *supra*.
[107] See, for instance, i, 308, 315; vii, 212, 393.
[108] See pp. 56-59 *supra*.

as Purchas customarily gives. From the beginning Milton was interested in all forms of religion. His reference in *The Doctrine and Discipline of Divorce*[109] to marriage, which is "worshipt like some Indian deity, when it can conferre no blessing upon us, but works more and more to our misery," may well stem from some such passage in *Pilgrimage* as Gilbert[110] quotes. And the same may be said of another prose allusion[111] to the sun to which "even to this day we learn that the peoples of the Indian Occident sacrifice with incense and with other ceremonial." In this connection Gilbert[112] reproduces two extracts from *Pilgrimes*.[113]

Finally, we may safely say that there are certain pages of Purchas that carry general discussions which very probably had their effect upon Milton. He would hardly have been unaware of the chapter in *Pilgrimage*[114] where "the question [is] discussed, whether Cathay and China be the same," the chapter which concludes "let every Reader judge as pleaseth him." And when, near the beginning of his great epic, he referred to "the secret top of *Oreb*, or of *Sinai*," he must have known that Purchas had a chapter entitled "Mount Sinai, Oreb, and the adjoyning parts of Arabia, described out of the foure Journals of Breidenbach, etc."[115]

---

[109] *Works*, III, 425. With this should be quoted a passage from the Second Defense (*Works*, VIII, 7): "The lower orders, stupefied by the wicked arts of priests, had not yet degenerated into a barbarism viler than what disgraces the Indians, dullest of mortals: for these merely worship as gods those malignant demons they are unable to put to flight."

[110] *Op.cit.*, p. 155.

[111] *Prolusions.* See *Works*, XII, 139.

[112] *Op.cit.*, pp. 156-157. Sun-worship by the West Indians was, however, a well-known practice. See R. R. Cawley, *Voyagers and Elizabethan Drama*, pp. 371-372.

[113] The passage in Commonplace Book (*Works*, XVIII, 158) about the natives of Congo rejecting Christianity because it forbade polygamy is fortunately placed for us by Milton himself as coming from Ralegh. Gilbert (*op.cit.*, pp. 90-91) quotes an interesting explanatory passage from Purchas.

[114] Pp. 342-347.

[115] *Pilgrimes*, II, 1376ff.

The problem as to whether he was inclined to use *Pilgrimage* or the more voluminous *Pilgrimes* is largely an academic one. There has been a

It has long been recognized that Milton made some use of George Sandys' *Relation of a Journey begun An. Dom. 1610.* Verity[116] is prepared to be quite dogmatic on the subject, declaring that the work "was certainly known to Milton" and that it was probably his "main authority for the topography of Palestine." There is no doubt that it was a very popular book for the time, editions appearing in 1615, 1621, 1627, 1632, 1637, 1652, and 1658. To be sure, the poet may have sensed, what has later been discovered, that Sandys was something of a Mandeville in that he was willing to accept what others gave him without bothering to verify. There is therefore in his pages much uncorroborated material which betrays his credulity and which would keep Milton from using him in any real sense as an authority. On the other hand, Sandys had a flair for what was notable and interesting,[117] not to say spectacular and strange; and his narrative may well have impressed the young poet. He does describe in detail some of the regions in which Milton was most interested, Italy and Greece, Egypt and the Holy Land. And he does retell with literary skill the old myths, quoting and translating liberally from the classics themselves. Under these circumstances we should expect to find Milton borrowing a striking detail here and there; and that is just

---

tendency by scholars to quote the former more often. What little evidence exists points rather to the latter. To take just one example, Milton's spelling "Atabalipa" is found in *Pilgrimes* (see IV, 1492ff.) whereas the earlier work has "Atabaliba" (see p. 718ff.). See also p. 20 *supra*.

Whiting finds Purchas underlying Milton's descriptions of some of the pagan divinities. (See *op.cit.*, esp. Chap. v.)

A study of Hakluyt returns to a large extent the same results. It is clear that Milton regarded his great collection in much the same light as Purchas, though at times one gets a pervasive sense of Hakluyt's presence in the poet's lines. With the plain in which a black bituminous gurge boils out from underground, the mouth of Hell (Bk. XII, ll. 41-42), Gilbert (p. 43) quotes a strikingly similar passage from *Principall Navigations*. And, as has been seen (cf. p. 99 *supra*), Hakluyt is closer than any to the poet's "Earths green Cape and verdant Isles" (Bk. VIII, l. 631), using "greene cape" (see Gilbert, p. 133), Milton's exact phrase.

[116] *Op.cit.*, pp. 383 and 646.

[117] See, for instance, his descriptions of the pyramids and the sphinx.

what we do find. Verity bases his own conclusions mainly on two passages, first the description of Moloch's rites both in the Nativity Ode and in *Paradise Lost*, Book 1;[118] and second, the account of Gaza and the amphitheatre which Samson destroyed.[119] In these instances there is a good possibility that Milton was actually recalling pages from the *Relation*. In general, it may be said that where he used Sandys he used him because the latter succeeded in revivifying for him some association which he already had with the classics or the Bible. He resorted to such books with somewhat the same purpose for which he went to Italy and wished to go to Sicily and Greece, that is to bring alive the materials he had been studying in classical and Biblical literature. Thus there can be no question that he was perfectly familiar with Pliny and his accounts of the pyramids. But the fact that Sandys described anew those phenomena, that he used much of Pliny's fascinating detail, and that he added his own observations made the poet view the monuments with fresh eyes. It is not even going too far to say that, when in the First Book[120] Milton was reaching for an example of the vain and presumptuous shows of man, and hit upon "the works of *Memphian Kings*," he was borrowing something of Sandys' disillusionment in referring contemptuously to men's "greatest Monuments of Fame."

[118] More recently Whiting (*op.cit.*, pp. 201-202) has pointed out similar analogies with passages in Ralegh, Purchas, and Fuller.

[119] See *Milton's Ode*, etc. (Pitt Press Series, Cambridge, 1931), p. 60; and *Samson Agonistes* (also Pitt Press Series, Cambridge, 1932), pp. xxviii and 130. As Verity acknowledges, Thomas Warton had earlier pointed out the connection between the Moloch passages and Sandys (see *Poetical Works*, Oxford and London, 1824, III, 370-371, note).

[120] Ll. 692-699.
In his identification of new Alcairo with old Memphis (Bk. 1, l. 718) we have merely another example of Milton's choosing to enrich his allusion with other associations. The fact that Sandys should deny the identification would, of course, have made no difference to the poet: "This hath made some erroniously affirme old Memphis to have bin the same with new Cairo" (see *A Relation*, p. 132).

Sandys[121] had after all referred to the pyramids as "the barbarous monuments of prodigality and vain-glory." The sentiment just suited Milton's mood when he wrote that passage in *Paradise Lost*.

Sandys' concern with the religion of Egypt was another interest shared by Milton. It will be recalled that besides the pagan deities of Palestine he introduces into the Nativity Ode,

> The brutish gods of *Nile* as fast,
> Isis and *Orus*, and the Dog *Anubis* hast (ll. 211-212).

And in the next stanza appears the most important of them all, Osiris.[122] One of the important sections of Sandys is devoted to the "Religion of the Aegyptians." And throughout his description of that part of the world the chief divinities continue to be mentioned. In one place,[123] for example, he gives pictorial representations of them in their brutish forms, among them, "the monster-Gods, Anubis barking." And elsewhere[124] he describes those closely associated with the religious practices, "They weare ... gownes with wide sleeves," a passage which recalls some lines in *Animadversions*[125] where Milton speaks of the "Priest of *Isis* in his lawne sleeves." These were, however, matters of fairly common knowledge. The same may be said for "the unshowr'd Grasse" of the Nativity Ode, in connection with which it has been customary to quote Sandys. Egypt's lack of rain was apt to be mentioned about as regularly as the Nile's inundations.[126]

The part of Sandys' *Travels* which might have fascinated

[121] *Relation*, p. 127.

[122] Osiris, Isis, and Orus reappear in *Paradise Lost* (Bk. i, ll. 478-481) "disguis'd in brutish forms."

[123] *Op.cit.*, p. 133.   [124] P. 110.   [125] *Works*, iii, 173.

[126] See R. R. Cawley, *Voyagers and Elizabethan Drama*, pp. 16-17. "Rain is very rare in this land (and that onely in winter)," wrote Thomas Fuller in *A Pisgah-Sight*, Bk. iv, p. 79.

Mention of Belus (Bk. i, l. 720) was likewise a commonplace, though Sandys does refer to him, as Verity says (see *op.cit.*, p. 396).

the poet more than any other would be the pages treating the Holy Land. Doubtless Sandys' seeming credulity[127] would at times have disturbed him, and the *Relation* may actually be responsible in part for the lines in which the poet expresses considerable skepticism about journeys to Palestine:

Here Pilgrims roam, that stray'd so farr to seek
In *Golgotha* him dead, who lives in Heav'n (Bk. III,
ll. 476-477).

Verity is probably justified in his fairly frequent references to Sandys in explanation of matters which concern the Holy Land. Certainly the allusion to Moloch's grove, "the pleasant Vally of *Hinnom*,"[128] is reminiscent of "the valley of *Gehinnon*" which is "planted with groves, and watered with fountaines."[129] Similarly, the juxtaposition of names a little later in connection with Dagon, who had reared his temple,

in *Azotus*, dreaded through the Coast
Of *Palestine*, in *Gath* and *Ascalon*,
And *Accaron* and *Gaza's* frontier bounds (Bk. I, ll, 464-466),

appears to have distinct echoes from a short passage in *A Relation*:[130] "Ten miles North of *Ascalon* along the shore stands *Azotus*: and eight miles beyond that *Acharon*, now places of no reckoning." And this is especially true when we note that "Ascalon. Azotus. Acharon." head the page in Sandys.

Perhaps the crucial passage—at least the passage most often cited—is the one which describes the Serbonian bog;

[127] Sandys identifies, apparently with the utmost confidence, the very spots where happened many of the incidents associated with Jesus' life.

[128] *P.L.*, Bk. I, ll. 403-404.

[129] See Verity, *op.cit.*, p. 384.

This is especially significant since the quotation comes from the same page (186) as the passage about Moloch's rites.

[130] P. 151.

These names appear in Sandys on the same page with his description of Dagon. He too is talking about Gaza: "Ten miles from *Gaza*, and neare unto the Sea, stands *Ascalon*."

Milton introduces it while telling about the frozen continent infested by hell's fallen angels:

> A gulf profound as that *Serbonian* Bog
> Betwixt *Damiata* and mount *Casius* old,
> Where Armies whole have sunk (Bk. ii, ll. 592-594).

The ultimate source of this, as was long ago pointed out, is in Diodorus Siculus.[131] But the question inevitably arises as to whether the Sicilian's account may not have been modified by some modern traveler before it found its way into *Paradise Lost*. Sandys' "modernization" is as follows:[132]

A little beneath is the lake *Sirbonis*. . . . A place to such as knew it not, in those times full of unsuspected danger. Then two hundred furlongs long; being but narrow, and bordered on each side with hils of sand, which borne into the water by the winds so thickned the same, as not by the eye to be distinguished from a part of the Continent: by meanes whereof whole armies have bene devoured. For the sands neare hand seeming firme, a good way entred slid farther off, and left no way of returning, but with a lingring cruelty swallowed the ingaged. . . . Close to this standeth the mountaine *Cassius*.

Sandys reproduces and conditions the old material in a way that might well have colored the poet's imagination.[133]

With a region so generally known as the Dead Sea one feels less safe in making any such assumption. Milton,[134] it will be recalled, connected his next devil-god with the "*Asphaltick* Pool," by which he means the Dead Sea. The one element which might justify us in seeing Sandys behind this passage is that *A Relation*[135] uses a similar identification: "that cursed lake *Asphalites* [sic]: so named of the *Bitumen* which it vomiteth."[136]

131 See Verity, *op.cit.*, p. 415. Diodorus' influence throughout Milton is considerable. See analysis by E. N. S. Thompson, sp, xvi, 161-163. Cf. also Whiting, *op.cit.*
132 *Op.cit.*, p. 137.
133 Whiting (*op.cit.*, p. 119) sees in the lines some influence by Ortelius.
134 *P.L.*, Bk. i, l. 411.   135 P. 141.
136 See Verity, *op.cit.*, p. 385.
While quoting Sandys, however, Verity reproduces a passage from

The type of conceivable borrowing represented by these last instances may be seen elsewhere. When dealing with a person so thoroughly trained in the classics as Milton, one must necessarily be cautious in reading into him some contemporary redaction. On the other hand, we should never exclude the possibility. The best example here is the famous story of Xerxes bridging the Hellespont, a story so effectively used by the poet in describing the causeway built by Sin and Death across Chaos to the system of the World:

> So, if great things to small may be compar'd,
> *Xerxes*, the Libertie of *Greece* to yoke,
> From *Susa* his *Memnonian* Palace high
> Came to the Sea, and over *Hellespont*
> Bridging his way, *Europe* with *Asia* joyn'd,
> And scourg'd with many a stroak th' indignant waves
> (Bk. x, ll. 306-311).

Nobody doubts that this is essentially Herodotus. But nobody, on the other hand, can read the version in Sandys[137] without a feeling that somehow the passage has its bearing on Milton, even if it was only to remind him of the story as he had read it earlier in the Greek:

It [the Hellespont] divideth *Europe* from *Asia*. . . . Here *Xerxes* . . . is said to have past over into *Greece* upon a bridge of boates. . . . Which when broken by tempests, he caused the sea to be beaten (as if sensible) with three hundred stripes.

One does not feel the same assurance in connection with the Charybdis passage near the close of Book Two.[138]

Thomas Blount's *Glossographia* (1656) which uses the same term. And in connection with the later reference (Bk. x, l. 298) he concedes that the name was "said to have been first given it by the historian Diodorus Siculus."

In his Map of Judah (*Pisgah-Sight*, pp. 264-265) Fuller has "Mare Mortuum . . . Lacus Asphaltitis."

[137] *Op.cit.*, p. 25.

Sandys' translation of Lucan's version (same page), "fretfull Hellespontus," has in it a strong suggestion of Milton's "indignant waves." Cf. also the translation, "durst joyne Europe to Asia," with Milton's "*Europe* with *Asia* joyn'd."

[138] Ll. 1019-1022.

A Growing Conscience

Sandys[139] had, to be sure, brought the old story "up-to-date" with a graphic description of his own experience. But Homer so dominates the passage that there seems scarcely to be room for anyone else. The same holds largely true for the famous lines about Proserpina and Enna in Book Four,[140] though Ortelius, as Whiting[141] suggests, may have played his part.

In the above analogies drawn between Milton and Sandys there is enough evidence to support Verity[142] in his conclusion that, because of what he was able to find, we may assume certain other connections which appeared but likely. Thus we are the more ready to accept Todd's early conjecture that the poet's "double-founted stream *Jordan*"[143] may well derive from *A Relation*:[144] "*Jordan* . . . seeming to arise from *Jor*, and *Dan*, two not far distant fountaines."[145]

---

[139] *A Relation*, pp. 247-248. Professor Bush (*Mythology and the Renaissance Tradition*, p. 259) points to Sandys' translation, "fell Charybdis."

[140] Ll. 268-272. Gilbert (*op.cit.*, p. 115) quotes or cites Ovid, Diodorus, and Claudian.

[141] *Op.cit.*, pp. 108-109.

[142] *Op.cit.*, p. 646.
Cf. also Marjorie Nicolson in *University of Toronto Quarterly*, vol. vii, 500-513 (July, 1938), where she draws the connection between Milton's Hell and the Phlegraean Fields as described by Sandys. See esp. pp. 508-513.

[143] *P.L.*, Bk. xii, ll. 144-145.

[144] P. 141. Slight corroborative testimony is to be found in the fact that the passage appears on the same page with Sandys' reference to "that cursed lake Asphalites." See p. 106 *supra*.
To show, however, what caution should be exercised in these matters, Fuller has a remarkably similar passage in *A Pisgah-Sight* (p. 106): "This is mount *Paneas*, wherein there is a deep hole or cave. . . . Herein also was an unsoundable spring of water, conceived by some to be the primitive fountain of *Jordan*. . . . But we are not to take notice where rivers are secretly conceived, but where they are visibly born: and therefore date the originall thereof from the apparent heads of *Jor* and *Dan*: which keeping themselves sole and single for a short time, are soon wedded together. And from the confluence of their names and streams, *Jordan* is begotten."
Furthermore, Whiting (*op.cit.*, pp. 59-60) quotes an apposite passage from Ralegh's History.

[145] The only conceivable reason for scholars' pointing out that both Milton and Sandys spell "Damasco" (see *A Relation*, pp. 124, 145, 172) is the negative one that the poet was not necessarily following the Italian romances.

A Growing Conscience

It happened that Thomas Fuller issued his *Pisgah-Sight of Palestine* in 1650 in plenty of time to be of use to Milton while he was composing *Paradise Lost*. It happens also that it was the sort of book that would appeal to him in many ways. Along with its reproduction of a considerable amount of Biblical material, it included other historical and pseudo-historical matter, besides geographical information which would be of special interest to the poet. Furthermore, many of Fuller's preoccupations and attitudes would have found a sympathetic audience in Milton. Fuller[146] bids his reader follow him, "so far as I follow the truth, at least the most probability grounded on Scripture, ancient Authors, and modern Travellers who have been eye-witnesses of the countrey." And one gets the impression from him of being taken on a personally conducted tour: "Let us now request the Reader, to climbe up the hills of *Abarim, Nebo*, and *Pisgah*."[147] Probably the very fact that *A Pisgah-Sight* appeared when it did and was the kind of book it was has made scholars prone to quote it in connection with Milton's poem. Verity includes a number of its passages, and more recently G. W. Whiting has shown that there is great likelihood that the work directly influenced certain lines in *Paradise Lost*. This applies not merely to the text but to the fairly numerous graphic maps[148] which Fuller includes. In light of the evidence that he has succeeded in presenting, Whiting's statement[149] that "probably Milton knew Fuller's *Pisgah-Sight*" is a modest one. We have always to remember, however, that the Bible, on which the book is largely based, was above all others the work which Milton knew best. And more-

---

[146] *Pisgah-Sight*, p. 48.
It is to be noticed that Fuller often refers to Sandys as his authority.
[147] *Op.cit.*, Bk. II, p. 63.
[148] The work could have come into the poet's hands two years before total blindness set in. E. N. S. Thompson (SP, XVI, 157-158) similarly analyzes a chart in Fuller's *Holy Warre* (1639) and shows how Milton might have used some of its details.
[149] *Op.cit.*, p. 102.

over, where matters of the Holy Land were concerned he was apt to resort to such authorities as Bochart's *Geographia Sacra*, Adrichomius' *Theatrum Terrae Sanctae* and *Urbis Hierosolimae Descriptio*, Josephus' *Antiquitates Judaicae*, and Breydenbach's *Peregrinatio in Terram Sanctam*. It is further to be noticed, as Whiting[150] says, that he was acquainted with charts so generously furnished by the Bibles.

With these various lines crossing and recrossing it is not easy to isolate those elements which might have suggested to the poet certain of his images. But every now and then the juxtaposition of words is so striking that we are almost driven to assume some dependence. For instance, as Whiting[151] shows, Milton's description of Rimmon,

> whose delightful Seat
> Was fair *Damascus*, on the fertil Banks
> Of *Abbana* and *Pharphar*, lucid streams (Bk. i, ll. 467-469),

recalls Fuller's characterization of the god as "an Idol of *Syria* whose principall Temple was in *Damascus*," and his reference to the rivers: "*Abanah* and *Pharphar* were highly beholden to *Naaman*, who preferred them *before all the waters of Israel*."[152] In the next line Fuller[153] asks, "But what if the water in the Cistern chance to be clearer then that in the Font?" It is not difficult to extend the list to include other concatenations of names which, to say the least, are suggestive. In *Samson Agonistes*, for example, Milton writes of,

> *Ecron, Gaza, Asdod*, and in *Gath* (l. 981).[154]

These names all appear in *A Pisgah-Sight*, all within two

[150] *Op.cit.*, p. 108.

[151] *Op.cit.*, p. 117.

[152] This last is, however, one of those places where one cannot help wondering whether anything besides the Bible was in the poet's mind.

[153] *Op.cit.*, Bk. iv, 7.

[154] Another example is to be found with the Paneas passage of Book Three (ll. 535-537), in connection with which Gilbert (*op.cit.*, p. 225) quotes a close parallel from *A Pisgah-Sight* (p. 106).

pages,[155] and all in an account of Samson. The Bible itself doubtless underlies the line,

The flowry Dale of *Sibma* clad with Vines (Bk. 1, l. 410);

but Gilbert[156] was quite right in going on to say that Fuller's map of the tribe of Reuben shows a conspicuous grapevine near "Shibmah." Whiting[157] goes still further and quotes from *A Pisgah-Sight*,[158] where the reader is taken "to *Sibmah*, so famous for her fruitfull vinyards." As if to justify the picture in his chart Fuller continues: "It seems in *Sibmah* there was some one signall vine eminent for greatness above the rest, or else that all her vines grew so close and uniform, that they resembled one entire and continued tree."

Studies have also been made of Milton's sources for his elaborate catalogue of fallen gods in Book One. Whiting[159] finds, for instance, that Milton was recalling a whole series of books: Diodorus, Plutarch's *Moralia*, Augustine's *De Civitate* (together with Vives' learned commentary), Hesiod, Purchas, and Ralegh, as well as Fuller. It is clear from these studies that *A Pisgah-Sight* must have played some part in the formation of Milton's conceptions. Fuller[160] has his own section devoted to "The Idols of the Jews," in which appear Moloch and Chemos, Baalim and Astoreth, Thammuz and Rimmon and Dagon, in fact most in the list of devil-gods which the poet has so elaborately described for us. In trying to discern Fuller's influence here, however, we should not for a moment forget that Purchas was, if anything, even more interested in the world's religions, that the subtitle of his book was actually "Relations of the World and the Religions Observed in All Ages,"[161] and

[155] Pp. 218-219.
[156] *Op.cit.*, p. 268. See *Pisgah-Sight*, p. 53.
[157] *Op.cit.*, p. 206.   [158] P. 66.
[159] *Op.cit.*, Chap. v ("Pagan Deities"), esp. pp. 201-214.
[160] *Op.cit.*, Bk. IV, 123ff.
[161] Actually in the original edition this part is printed to dwarf what is usually accepted as the main title.

that he also has a list of pagan divinities which in some
details is remarkably like Milton's. While describing Dagon,
for instance, he has "captived Arke,"[162] which recalls Milton's "Captive Ark"[163] in the same connection. But Fuller
also weaves himself in and out of the poetic description.
With this very figure of Dagon, indeed, Milton probably
recalled in detail, not merely the Biblical account but the
versions in both Purchas[164] and Fuller.[165] The latter may
have impressed him partly by a clever jingle he wrote about
the god.[166] After the Bible, Whiting tends to trace the lines
on Dagon about equally to Ralegh and Purchas. Towards
the end of his account he quotes the Fuller jingle with the
comment attached. Far more suggestive, however, are the
two pages of pictures representing Jewish idols in *A Pisgah-
Sight*.[167] Milton's lines are as follows:

> Next came one
> Who mourn'd in earnest, when the Captive Ark
> Maim'd his brute Image, head and hands lopt off
> In his own Temple, on the grunsel edge,
> Where he fell flat, and sham'd his Worshipers:
> *Dagon* his Name, Sea Monster, upward Man
> And downward Fish (Bk. i, ll. 457-463).

There is not a single element in this whole description
which does not appear in Fuller's engraving. Here is the
captive ark clearly portrayed, here is the maimed image
with head and hands cleanly cut off and with the body lying
prone right on the threshold. Here too are the worshipers
looking very much abashed. And the monster is human to
the waist and below that a fish. We have here clearly an
instance where the Bible did *not* furnish Milton with all or

---

[162] *Pilgrimage*, p. 79. [163] *P.L.*, Bk. i, l. 458.
[164] See *Pilgrimage*, p. 79.
[165] Whiting (*op.cit.*, pp. 210-211) quotes appropriately from Ralegh.
[166] *Pisgah-Sight*, Bk. ii, 220.
[167] See Bk. iv, 120-121. Fuller, like Milton, associates Dagon with
Azotus: "Here *Jonathan* . . . burns *Azotus*; and the Temple of *Dagon*"
(*op.cit.*, p. 219).

even most of his suggestions.[168] Granted the poet's natural
interests and the engraving's own remarkable qualities of
vividness, it is quite conceivable that Milton might have
remembered its details over the years.

There is no need to pause for more than a few minutes
on Ortelius. His connection with Milton has already been
made the subject of a thorough study.[169] A. S. Cook[170] long
ago emphasized the fact that "Namancos" in *Lycidas* may
well derive from Ortelius. And Miss Lockwood[171] showed
how the poet rested on the cosmographer's authority in
placing "that *Nyseian* Ile." There is no question that Milton, like most of his well-informed contemporaries, looked
upon Ortelius as something of an authority. He was in a
sense a purveyor of the old legends, and it may well be that
he did his share in coloring those legends for poetic use.[172]
For example, he gave Amalthea, if not a name, at least a
local habitation.[173] Whiting[174] has gone on to argue that
Ortelius may well lie behind such matters as the "*Tyrrhene*
shore" and "*Circes* Iland" of *Comus*, as well as the "faire
field of *Enna*" in *Paradise Lost*. In referring to the doubt
in Milton's own mind as to the position of Ur, Professor
Gilbert[175] refers to a specific map in Ortelius, the one showing the Journeys of Abraham. It is true that there has been
some tendency to cite him as source where others are at
least as likely. This may be due in part to the external
evidence; in *Animadversions* Milton[176] warned his reader

[168] Cf. I Samuel 5:2-5.
  I am publishing separately some material showing how Milton used
more details from that same "Pantheon" of Fuller for his other pagan
deities.
  [169] See G. W. Whiting, *Milton's Literary Milieu*, Chapter III, "The Use
of Maps."
  [170] MLR, II, 124ff.
  [171] MLN, XXI, 86. See *P.L.*, Bk. IV, ll. 275-276.
  [172] This applies to Biblical as well as classical story.
  [173] See Miss Lockwood's article, cited above.
  [174] *Op.cit.*, pp. 100-101 and 108-109. There is a good chance that
Biblical names were similarly taken from the pages of *Theatrum*.
  [175] *Op.cit.*, pp. 306-307.   [176] *Works*, III, 138.

not to "trouble *Ortelius*" when he was seeking the silly countries which Bishop Hall invented for his *Mundus Alter et Idem*. But there would seem to be little justification for quoting any one source in connection with the northeast winds that blow Sabean odors from the spicy shore of Araby the Blest.[177] Then, Milton wrote of the sea that separates,

Calabria from the hoarce *Trinacrian* shore (Bk. II, l. 661).

And before him admittedly Ortelius[178] had referred to "Sicilia Sive Trinacria." But Sandys[179] had also recorded of Sicily that "it beareth the forme of a triangle, and was first called *Trinacria* of her three Promontories." Both Milton and Ortelius wrote of the vast African empire of "Negus." But so, as it happens, did Heylyn[180] and Leo.[181]

There are certain books of travel, available to Milton, which we might have expected him to use more than he appears to have done. One of those was Leo Africanus' *Geographical Historie of Africa*. There had been what for the time was an excellent translation by John Pory in 1600. And evidence from the Commonplace Book[182] exists to prove that Milton knew of the work. In connection with many of the African places which the poet mentions Gilbert quotes passages from Leo—such places as Fez, Sus, Tremisen, Niger, Atlas, Marocco, and Algiers. But these quotations are professedly nothing more than explanatory. If the evidence of spelling counts for anything—and it appears to do so—Milton's familiarity with the book was not close.[183]

---

[177] *P.L.*, Bk. IV, ll. 161-163. And see pp. 71-72 *supra*.

[178] *Op.cit.*, Antwerp, 1612, p. xxix.

[179] *Relation*, p. 234.   [180] See p. 15 *supra*.

[181] *History and Description of Africa*, 1896, I, 32.

[182] *Works*, XVIII, 139. His knowledge came through Purchas. See p. 86 *supra*.

[183] Linschoten's *Discours of Voyages into the Easte and West Indies* is somehow another book which one might have expected to find more often in *Paradise Lost*. There was a very good English edition of it in 1598. It

A Growing Conscience

Of the travel books which Milton did use, however, one can say that he held, in each case, fairly definite conceptions about the nature of its usefulness. He regarded Heylyn in quite another sense from Purchas; and this was due not only to the vast difference in size of the two works but to the manner in which the authors wrote. Heylyn stood alone as providing equally both basic materials and a philosophy or attitude. Fuller, on the other hand, was apt to suggest, at times, merely a vivid and exotic detail. Preacher Purchas expressed doctrines which undoubtedly appealed to Milton, but actually his more important function was to furnish the poet with occasional incidents recalled from the leisurely pages of his *Pilgrimes*. George Sandys, translator of Ovid, helped Milton to give a sense of modernness to classical geography. Certainly by the time he came to write *Paradise Lost* Milton was fully conscious of the particular way in which each of these writers might contribute to his poem.

---

is tempting to read him behind the elaborate fig-tree passage of Book Nine (ll. 1101-1114). But the picture is almost endlessly complicated by the existence of similar passages in Pliny and Purchas and Gerard's *Herball* (see pp. 98-99 *supra*). Gilbert (*op.cit.*, pp. 153-155) quotes from Linschoten to illustrate the lines where Milton describes Eve's plucking fruits of paradise to entertain Raphael (Bk. v, ll. 331-344).

As with Ortelius the geographical matter in Diodorus and Ralegh has been examined at some length by Professor Whiting in *Milton's Literary Milieu* (see esp. Chap. ii, "Three Histories of the World"). In connection with the former at least, it is noticeable that a considerable amount of the material may about as well stem from elsewhere. This applies to such matters as Serbonian bog, Sabean odors, the Asphaltic Pool, and the circuit of Nineveh.

CHAPTER VI

ANCIENT AND MODERN

Wʜᴀᴛ was transpiring in that middle period of Milton's career accounts fully for the difference in type of geographic reference we find him using. As blindness came on, he was obviously resorting more and more to the "digest" sort of book, was reading, or was having read to him, the more summary pages of a Heylyn rather than the more leisurely ones of a Purchas or a Hakluyt. But there is a factor of even greater importance to observe. The very nature of his allusion changes. There is something less stereotyped and conventional about it, something more specific and "modern." In *Comus*,[1] for example, he will speak of "the nice Morn on th' *Indian* steep," whereas in *Paradise Lost*[2] he has localized by referring to "the Iles of *Ternate* and *Tidore*." The sorcerers of *In Quintum Novembris*[3] are placed in Etruria. Partly through his researches for *A Brief History*[4] Milton learned that sorcerous witches were regularly associated with Lapland. In *Paradise Lost*[5] the horrible Night-Hag is represented as coming to dance "with Lapland Witches."[6] The Seventh Latin Elegy[7] makes it the *Parthian* horseman who wins his fight by shooting over his shoulder as he flees. But the travelers associated the practice with Tartars,[8] and in *Paradise Lost* Milton follows them:

As when the *Tartar* from his *Russian* Foe
By *Astracan* over the Snowie Plaines
Retires (Bk. x, ll. 431-433).

[1] L. 139.
[2] Bk. ii, ll. 638-639.
[3] *Latin Poems*, p. 123.
[4] *Works*, x, 361.
[5] Bk. ii, ll. 662-665.
[6] See pp. 80-81 *supra*.
[7] *Works*, i, 217.
[8] *Inter alia*, Hakluyt, *op.cit.*, i, 158, and Purchas, *op.cit.*, xi, 362. Spenser likewise has Tartars in this connection. See discussion, R. R. Cawley, *op.cit.*, pp. 200-201. See also pp. 53-54 *supra*.

The Tartar himself ranges over Milton's pages from the stock character of romance on his wondrous horse of brass,[9] to the belligerent figure of *A Brief History* in almost continual warfare with the Russian,[10] to the "roving *Tartar*" of *Paradise Lost*.[11]

In this whole consideration, however, one factor should not be overlooked. Milton's general tendency might well be to use the newer material provided him by recent, or comparatively recent, travelers. But those travelers might be the very ones to perpetuate old misconceptions. The pages of Heylyn and Hexham, of Hakluyt and Purchas, even of Sandys and Fuller are a fascinating amalgam of the new and old. Quite often, it is true, the poet was aware when he borrowed something which was no longer accepted as fact. Quite as often the traveler gave him authority for continuing to think it was a fact. The Ancients thus were substantiated by the Moderns, who repeated their stories and their theories without bothering to question their truth. This cuts both ways. The poet has a richer storehouse from which to draw his images, and those images are the fresher, the more current, perhaps the more credible because a contemporary has reproduced something ancient almost as if it were within his own personal experience. This cannot help giving a sense of immediacy to the allusion, both in the way the poet uses it and in the way the reader receives it.

What has been said applies to the Bible naturally as well as to the classics. Examples within the poem are indeed numerous. Diodorus may have been one of the chief mediums by which ancient legends came down into seventeenth-century England. But Diodorus was rendered up-to-date, so to speak, by Sandys and Fuller and Ortelius, three of Milton's prime favorites. The outworn story of Amalthea is given new life when Ortelius justifies Milton in his plac-

---

[9] *Il Penseroso*, ll. 114-115.
[10] See pp. 52-53 *supra*.
[11] Bk. III, l. 432.

ing of the story.[12] Diodorus purveyed many of the old
stories about the Dead Sea, was thought to be the one to
give it the name of "Lake *Asphaltites*."[13] But Sandys[14] was
to write of "that cursed lake *Asphalites* [sic]: so named of
the *Bitumen* which it vomiteth." This applies also to the
notorious Dead Sea apples which have furnished poetry with
such a convenient figure. Josephus had written his own
description; but Ralegh[15] had continued it:

And it is found by Experience, that those Pomegranates, and
other Apples, or Oranges, which do still grow on the Banks
of this cursed Lake, do look fair, and are of good Colour on the
Out-side; but being cut, have nothing but Dust within.

Ralegh's contemporaries, who were by chance also Milton's,
would read with different eyes such a passage as the following and would better understand the bitter experience of
Satan's followers:

> greedily they pluck'd
> The Frutage fair to sight, like that which grew
> Neer that bituminous Lake where *Sodom* flam'd
> (Bk. x, ll. 560-562).

The very fact that a modern scholar[16] should have stated
with some positiveness that he believed George Sandys'
Relation "was Milton's main authority for the topography
of Palestine" is significant. If Verity is right—and it is
likely he is—then Milton rested partly on Sandys' book
when he described Gaza and the building in which Samson's
catastrophe takes place, as well as when he told of the rites
of Moloch.[17] Herodotus had recounted in graphic detail
how the angry Xerxes had scourged with three hundred
lashes the Hellespont, which had presumed to destroy his
bridge of ships. Sandys retells the story as if it had happened
yesterday. It is likely that both Milton and many of his

---

[12] See L. E. Lockwood, MLN, XXI, 86.
[13] Cf. Verity, *op.cit.*, p. 597. [14] *Relation*, p. 141.
[15] Quoted by Whiting, *op.cit.*, p. 58.
[16] See Verity, *op.cit.*, p. 646. [17] See p. 103 *supra*.

contemporary readers were aware of the retelling in connection with the passage where the poet compares Xerxes'
great bridge to the devils' causeway.[18] When, in connection
with Moloch, Milton[19] refers to his having made "his Grove
the pleasant Vally of *Hinnom,*" he had of course the Biblical
passage in mind. But Scripture says nothing of the grove
of Hinnom, whereas Sandys[20] wrote: "We descended into
the valley of Gehinnon. . . . This valley is but streight, now
serving for little use; heretofore most delightfull, planted
with groves, and watered with fountaines." The Bible
might scatter somewhat indiscriminately through its pages
such names as Ascalon, Azotus, and Acharon. But it may
have been left to Sandys to suggest just that form which
makes such magnificent alchemy of Milton's lines on Dagon.
It suited the poet's purpose in *Paradise Regained* to describe the disgusting Tiberius:

> This Emperour hath no Son, and now is old,
> Old, and lascivious, and from *Rome* retir'd
> To *Capreae* an Island small but strong
> On the *Campanian* shore, with purpose there
> His horrid lusts in private to enjoy,
> Committing to a wicked Favourite
> All publick cares (Bk. iv, ll. 90-96).

Here again it is hard to believe that Sandys' version[21] did
not have some impact upon the poetic rendering:

We passed between this cape [of Minerva] and Caprae, an island distant three miles from the same, small and rocky. . . .
Tyberius made Caprae, by his cruelty and lusts, both infamous
and unhappy; who hither withdrawing from the affairs of the
Common-wealth . . . hence sent his Mandates of death.

The very way in which Sandys presented even so well
known a phenomenon as the pyramids may indeed have

---

[18] See p. 107 *supra.*
[19] *P.L.*, Bk. i, ll. 403-404.
[20] *Relation*, p. 186.
[21] Quoted by Gilbert, *op.cit.*, pp. 73-74. In 1621 ed. of the *Relation*,
p. 252.

impressed Milton so that the tendency of his own attitude
was partially determined.

This is an attitude which extends far beyond the poet's
relationship with any single traveler; it colors his approach
to travel literature as a whole. For him an important part
of the function of that literature was, not merely that it
corrected outworn preconceptions but that it continued
those preconceptions while modifying them by additions
of its own. Substantially this is what has happened to
theories of the Terrestrial Paradise. When scholars have
finished arguing as to whether the conception depends most
on the Bible, on Josephus, on Mandeville, or even on Ralegh,
they will be driven to concede that the travelers' accounts
had much to do with molding the theory.[22] The same is
naturally more true still of the Isles of the Blest and the
Fortunate Islands, and the rationalization that took place
in the late Middle Ages and the Renaissance. Ophir under-
goes a like modification. The story of Solomon's gold, stemming originally from the Bible, found its setting constantly
changed. One theory held that Sofala in East Africa was
the actual site. In Milton's reference, "*Sofala* thought *Ophir*,"
there is the implication that other places contended for the
honor. Actually this particular hypothesis appears to have
been advanced by Ortelius though, as we have seen, it may
have been Heylyn[23] who called Milton's attention to the
fact: "This Country [Sofala] for its abundance of *Gold* and
Ivory, is by some thought to be that land of *Ophir*, to
which *Solomon* sent; and of this opinion *Ortelius* in his
Thesaurus was the first Author."

Similarly one is justified in seeing Heylyn behind a passage which has been discussed in another connection.[24] It
is a modernization of the legend of Choaspes being "the

22 Cf. R. R. Cawley, *Unpathed Waters*, pp. 20-31.
23 *Cosmographie*, IV, 75. See pp. 97-98 *supra*.
24 See p. 31 *supra*.

drink of none but Kings."[25] The story must have been well known because it finds a place in Herodotus and Solinus as well as in Pliny. Heylyn[26] sensed the tale's worth and wrote that the river was "of so pure a stream, that the great *Persian* Kings would drink of no other water." Moreover, theories about Hell-mouth had been brought straight down through the Middle Ages from classical times. As it happens, Milton resorts to the conception in a passage fundamentally Biblical. The "mightie Hunter" (Nimrod) of Book XII[27] finds a plain wherein a black bituminous gurge boils out from under ground, "the mouth of Hell." The passage is full of the Biblical account of Babel. But "the mouth of Hell" seems to provide a different element, coming originally from the classics. How both Bible and classics may be modified is shown by the following passage in Hakluyt:[28] "By the river Euphrates two dayes journey from Babylon at a place called Ait, in a field neere unto it, is a strange thing to see: a mouth that doth continually throwe foorth against the ayre boyling pitch with a filthy smoke, which pitch doth runne abroad into a great field which is alwayes full thereof. The Moores say that it is the mouth of hell."

Once we recognize this as a general tendency in Milton, we become aware that certain uses which have been construed as archaizing may in fact not be archaizing in any strict sense at all. "Hydaspes"[29] has been set down as the classical name of an Indian stream. But Heylyn[30] speaks of the river as if it were the Ganges or the Rhine: "The famous Rivers *Indus, Hidaspis* . . . have their first beginnings." Similarly "Paneas"[31] may be, as Verity says, a later Greek

---

[25] *P.R.*, Bk. III, ll. 288-289.　　[26] *Cosmographie*, III, 162.
[27] L. 33ff.
[28] Quoted by Gilbert, *op.cit.*, p. 43.
[29] *P.L.*, Bk. III, l. 436.
[30] *Cosmographie*, III, 140. Cf. pp. 90-91 *supra*.
[31] *P.L.*, Bk. III, l. 535.

name of Dan; but it was a Greek name familiarly used by
Fuller:[32] "Amongst the mountains of Libanus, we meet
with one of eminent note. . . . This is Mount Paneas."
Ptolemy called the Chinese (or China) "Sinae." But it was
probably Heylyn[33] who directed many people's attention to
the fact that Ptolemy had done so. Milton's references to the
whale belong in a slightly different though allied category.
One gets the impression that they involve old and new preconceptions at the same time. In the most important allusion of all, the one where Satan is compared to a leviathan
slumbering on the Norway foam,[34] there are doubtless elements of the Physiologus as well as the Bible. But there is
just as probably a recollection of the passage in Olaus Magnus' *Compendious History of the Goths*, and of the accounts
in Hakluyt which we know he had been reading when he
composed *A Brief History of Moscovia*.[35]

There are of course cases where the modern travelers in
no sense modified a reputation which had been established
by the classics or the Bible. Their function here was merely
to perpetuate, at most to give some impression of the reputation's continuing to exist in the seventeenth century. Babylon and Cairo—and when Milton mentioned the latter, one
usually gets the feeling that he has old Memphis in mind—
are not infrequently spoken of as if their luxury was almost
perennial. And the same holds equally true of the whole of
Egypt and Assyria. For the reader of Milton's day tables
"heaped even to Persian splendor"[36] had special significance
because of the way some of their own contemporaries had
described that splendor. The Sabean odors of Araby the
Blest go back at least to Diodorus. But it is a matter of
consequence that Renaissance travelers were similarly impressed with the experience.

[32] Quoted by Gilbert, *op.cit.*, p. 225.
[33] *Cosmographie*, 1670, p. 864. See *P.L.*, Bk. XI, l. 390.
[34] Bk. I, l. 200ff.   [35] See pp. 50-51, note 36 *supra*.
[36] *Works*, XII, 235. In *Prolusions*.

In all of this one should not for a moment overlook the crucial role played by the maps. Milton resorted to them constantly in his eagerness to get his details as accurate as was consistent with the exigencies of poetry. An important part of his theory of education[37] consisted in the pupil's learning "in any modern Author, the use of the Globes, and all the Maps; first with the old names, and then with the new." And cartographers like Ortelius helped him in placing outlying regions which he had occasion to mention. It helped even that Ortelius had been specific about the wanderings of Ulysses.[38] Professor Whiting[39] has shown how the lines in which the architect of Pandemonium is thrown out of heaven on to Lemnos may well be a reflection of a passage in Ortelius, which in its turn is a reflection of the *Iliad*. Some of the very names from the Bible itself were in all likelihood suggested to Milton by the maps in *Theatrum*,[40] at least in the combination in which they are found. And this applies to *Paradise Regained* and *Samson Agonistes* as well as to *Paradise Lost*. Fuller's charts were equally helpful, especially when they were supplemented by his running commentary. There is picturesqueness both in the way Fuller represents the Biblical scenes pictorially and in the way he describes them. Jacob's dream, with the angels ascending and descending, is graphically portrayed in the Map of Benjamin, and Fuller's description of the incident bears a strong resemblance to Milton's lines.[41] Whiting[42] has all but proved that the list of winds which the poet gives in Book x[43] comes from Jansson's *Novus Atlas*, which, as it happens, is the one about which Milton so carefully inquired. In 1656 he had written to his friend Peter Heimbach, thanking him for having ascertained the price of a certain new Atlas:[44]

[37] *Works*, iv, 283. [38] See Whiting, *op.cit.*, pp. 100-101.
[39] *Op.cit.*, p. 101. [40] *Ibid.*, pp. 111 and 114.
[41] See Whiting, *op.cit.*, p. 115. In *A Pisgah-Sight* the Map of Benjamin is at pp. 238-239 and the account at p. 248. See *P.L.*, Bk. iii, ll. 510-515.
[42] *Op.cit.*, pp. 121-122. [43] Ll. 699-706.
[44] *Works*, xii, 83-85.

"Be good enough, pray, to take so much farther trouble for me as to be able to inform me, when you return, how many volumes there are in the complete work, and which of the two issues, that of Blaeu or that of Jansen, is the larger and more correct." In light of this obviously deep interest in maps it is rather surprising to find Verity[45] losing the edge of an allusion when he construes,

> To the Winds they set
> Thir corners, when with bluster to confound
> Sea, Aire, and Shoar (Bk. x, ll. 664-666),

as "their respective quarters." Clearly Milton has in mind the old maps with the four heads at four corners visibly blowing down upon the earth. It is the same, in reverse so to speak, with a passage in the Second Book[46] where the four cherubim proclaim the dissolution of the Stygian Council. Obviously *Ezekiel* is in the poet's mind; just as obviously the maps are there too.

It was Milton's close knowledge of the maps that made him capable of correcting others. He scolds[47] an unsuspecting minister who, he finds, develops his argument, "not without Geographical and Historical mistakes: as page 29, *Suevia* the German dukedom, for *Suecia* the Northern Kingdom." And one way in which he can overcome Salmasius is in his superior knowledge of maps and globes. In the *Defensio*[48] he holds the Frenchman up to scorn for having visualized a globe that never was on sea or land. The same accuracy which he demanded from others he tried to exemplify in his own works. It is doubtful whether any poet ever made a more serious attempt to get his details right. Milton is the best evidence we have that there is no inconsistency between great poetry and scrupulous accuracy in detail.

---

[45] *Op.cit.*, p. 606.   [46] Ll. 516-518.
[47] *Works*, VI, 157. "Brief Notes on a Sermon." The corrected minister was Matthew Griffith; the sermon was preached in 1660 and published in the same year.
[48] *Works*, VII, 407.

It is remarkable in how many instances of geographic fact where it was thought he had been proved to be wrong —in how many of those cases he has turned out to be right, at least as judged by the best authorities of his day. The difficulty about the sweet air of Arabia being blown by a northeast wind has already been explained as completely resolved.[49] The flight of the vulture "on *Imaus* bred"[50] making for Ganges and on his way flying over "Sericana" long gave trouble to note-writers. But Verity[51] showed how so good an authority as Hexham's Mercator pictured the country in such a way that a bird flying between those two points would naturally fly over the northwest plains of the Chinese Empire represented by Sericana. When Milton[52] placed the scene of Charlemagne's fall "by Fontarabbia," E. H. Marshall[53] advanced to his defense by pointing to a Spanish writer, Mariana, who does say that the Emperor's forces were routed there. What Marshall brings in rather incidentally carries more weight than his main argument; that is, Milton may be using "by" in the loose sense. He does so elsewhere; for instance, he puts Samarchand "by *Oxus*" when he almost certainly knew from his source that the city was at considerable remove from the river.[54] Masson called attention to Milton's care in making Satan come to Ganges before Indus.[55] R. C. Browne[56] indicated his accuracy in describing Athenian landmarks in *Paradise Regained*. And Miss Lockwood[57] demonstrated how, in placing the "*Nyseian* Ile," he followed Ortelius in almost meticulous detail. It is true that in the long range of his works there are slips; but they usually come at places where

[49] Cf. pp. 71-72 *supra*.
[50] *P.L.*, Bk. III, ll. 431-438.
[51] *Op.cit.*, pp. 683-684.
[52] *P.L.*, Bk. I, ll. 586-587.
[53] NQ, Ser. VII, no. XII, pp. 456-457.
[54] *P.L.*, Bk. XI, l. 389. See p. 12 *supra*.
[55] *P.L.*, Bk. IX, l. 82.
[56] Cf. his edition of Milton's *English Poems*, II, 315. See *P.R.*, Bk. IV, l. 240ff.
[57] MLN, XXI, 86. See *P.L.*, Bk. IV, ll. 275-276.

the requirements of poetry justify them. He will on occasion link Delos and Samos as being "amidst the *Cyclades*";[58] what Ovid had joined together, Milton would not put asunder. He confuses Susa with Nineveh;[59] he identifies Tarsus with Tarshish.[60] But these are the rare exceptions, and they are, as can be judged, inconsequential.

Generally speaking, Milton made far more of an effort than most poets to keep "up-to-date." His Commonplace Book has many quotations and paraphrases showing how he culled the latest information. Purchas apprizes him of the Indian custom in Sumatra of chewing "an hearb calld Arecca betula." From Leo Africanus he learns about Numidian poets. Sir Walter Ralegh puts him *au courant* with missionary problems in the Congo.[61] He shows himself to be aware of the great argument over the Nile's true source. He is deeply interested, as shown not merely by *A Brief History* but by his other prose and poetry as well, in the project of the Northeast Passage. And he is interested too in Ralegh and his discovery of the large, rich, and beautiful empire of Guiana. The American Indian finds a place, partly for his sacrifice to the sun-god[62] and partly for his "featherd Cincture."[63] Even so forbidding a region as Siberia, recently explored by Russian travelers, gets his attention. And he notices the nefarious practices of Algiers pirates. The "canie Waggons light"[64] driven by the Chinese

[58] *P.L.*, Bk. v, ll. 264-265.   [59] See First Latin Elegy.
[60] See *S.A.*, l. 715.   [61] *Works*, XVIII, 132, 139, 158.
[62] *Works*, XII, 139. In *Prolusions*. Gilbert (*op.cit.*, pp. 156-157) quotes appropriately from Purchas. His official position once more put him in contact with conditions in the West. If the Declaration Against Spain is his, and the Columbia editors think so, he made quite a study of Spaniards' mistreatment of Indians and their arrogance towards the English colonizers (see *Works*, XIII, 511ff.). And he undoubtedly translated with great relish the following articles, which appear here in their recent translation: "Englishmen were the first to plant colonies upon the continent of North America, and to maintain them there from the district of Virginia stretching far to the south from the 37th degree of North Latitude all the way up to Newfoundland and the 52nd degree." (*Works*, XVIII, 105-107.)
[63] *P.L.*, Bk. IX, l. 1117.   [64] *P.L.*, Bk. III, ll. 437-439.

over the barren plains of Sericana are clearly an attempt on the poet's part to use a circumstance not only striking but contemporary. When in *Paradise Regained*[65] he refers to the "utmost *Indian* Isle *Taprobane*," it is probable he has Sumatra in mind rather than the older identification with Ceylon.[66]

A recent critic[67] stresses the immediacy of Milton's geographical allusions, and comments that there is nothing bookish about them. This is due of course to his ability to make us feel that he had been in a place when he had not, that we were there when he had been. There are probably many more instances of this latter condition than have been suspected. The stock example to cite is the Fesole-Valdarno-Vallombrosa passage. But that surely is only one among many. We have here, of course, entered the realm of conjecture. Some have discerned St. Peter's behind Pandemonium. The great church had been dedicated only a few years before Milton reached Rome, and the conjecture is very probably justified. He is, moreover, fond of describing mountains; the lines in Book II,

> As when from mountain tops the dusky clouds
> Ascending, while the North wind sleeps, o'respread
> Heavn's chearful face, the lowring Element
> Scowls ore the dark'nd lantskip Snow, or showre
>   (ll. 488-491)

have, to be sure, something Virgilian about them. But at the same time they give the impression of a personal experience. It is well known that returning from Italy Milton crossed the Pennine Alps. Again the "flaming Mount, whose top brightness had made invisible"[68] recalls the Bible. But it can hardly help suggesting Vesuvius, which had erupted

---

[65] Bk. IV, l. 75.
[66] See G. W. Whiting, RES, XIII, 209-212.
[67] Sir William Foster. See "Milton and India," TLS, April 6, 1933, p. 248.
[68] *P.L.*, Bk. V, ll. 598-599.

only shortly before Milton reached Naples and which undoubtedly had been described to him by eyewitnesses. When
Satan looks down upon the system of the world, he is compared to a scout who discovers,

> The goodly prospect of some forein land
> First seen, or some renownd Metropolis
> With glistering Spires and Pinnacles adornd,
> Which now the Rising Sun guilds with his beams
> (Bk. III, ll. 548-551).

Verity conjectures that Milton was here recalling one of the
cities of his Italian tour, specifically mentions Florence, and
then "yet more likely, Rome." In light of the correspondent
passage where the Tuscan artist views the moon from "the
top of *Fesole*," it seems more likely that he has rather in
mind the unforgettable view over Florence at sunrise from
the slopes of Fiesole. Finally, one gets the definite impression in the accurate record of Athenian places which he
gives in *Paradise Regained*,[69] the olive grove of Academe,
the flowery hill Hymettus, Ilissus and its whispering stream,
the Lyceum and the painted Stoa, Socrates' "Tenement,"
that the poet is setting down just those things which he most
looked forward to seeing on the visit which never took place.

Allied with this tendency to resort at times to his own
personal experience is his introduction of prejudices against
foreign nations. Probably the outstanding example of this
last is to be found in connection with the Turk. In all of
Milton's works, prose or poetry, there is scarcely a good
word for the Turk. He is primarily, of course, the "foe of
Christendome," and his religion is "the Mahometan superstition." Milton probably learned most about him from
Knolles' mammoth History,[70] from Sandys' very unflatter-
ing account, and just possibly from Andrew Moore's *Com-*

---

[69] Bk. IV, l. 244ff.
[70] *The Generall Historie of the Turkes*, by Richard Knolles, London,
1603. The book's popularity may be judged by the number of editions:
1603, 1610, 1621, 1631, and 1638.

pendious History of the Turks (1660). The Turk is customarily represented as a tyrant, ignorant[71] and cruel.[72] "A Turkish Tyranny" referred to in *Eikonoklastes* was proverbial. Milton's most intimate knowledge of the race came through his official position since he was called upon to devise or draft letters protesting the abuse by Turks of British seamen.[73] All in all, the tendency went so far in him that he called Satan a Sultan,[74] and he was apt to use in connection with the devils such words of Turkish association as "thir dark *Divan.*"[75]

There is another poetic approach of Milton's which, in its way, is more important than any so far discussed. Difficult to define exactly, it might go under the term *objectification* —that is, the mention of some highly specific place which has the effect of bringing out the picture often with the magic of a stereoscope. Usually Milton uses this approach in some passage where he is dealing with materials which are essentially traditional. Theories of a Terrestrial Paradise had abounded ever since the Old Testament was composed. But when the poet sought places to compare with his own "Paradise of *Eden,*"[76] he chose as one, "Mount *Amara,* though this by som suppos'd true Paradise." The very mention of little-known Amara, together with such impressive details as the Abassin Kings' issue, the shining rock and the "whole dayes journey high," serves to bring the picture forward in a way that makes it memorable. The same may be said for his mention of places even less well known. In a passage[77] in which he is describing some of the

[71] "What can we say if our opponents put before us the argument that the modern Turks, ignorant of all literature, have obtained the mastery of affairs widely throughout the opulent kingdoms of Asia?" *Works,* XII, 271. In *Prolusions.*

[72] "If an Englishman forgetting all Laws, human, civil and religious, offend against life and liberty, . . . he is no better then a Turk, a Saracin, a Heathen." *Works,* V, 21. In *Tenure.*

[73] *Works,* XIII, 195, 499.   [74] *P.L.,* Bk. I, l. 348.
[75] *P.L.,* Bk. x, l. 457.   [76] *P.L.,* Bk. IV, l. 268ff.
[77] *P.L.,* Bk. x, l. 681ff.

conventional events succeeding the fall, Milton introduces
with an effect almost startling first "Estotiland" and then
"Norumbega," regions with which only the best informed
were familiar at all. With the latter he combines "*Samoed
shoar,*" another modernizing allusion. The words seem to
stand right out on the page, almost as if they had been
printed in rubrics. But in the way in which he uses them,
the terms, instead of calling attention to themselves, have
the effect of lifting the whole passage into relief. In some
other lines[78] which also have to do with the fall he accom-
plishes nearly the same result. This time he is talking, not
about the world in general but about man in particular.
Adam and Eve are seeking wherewith to cover "this new
commer, Shame." Ever since the Bible[79] had told how "the
eyes of them both were opened, and they knew that they
were naked; and they sewed fig leaves together, and made
themselves aprons," there had been speculation as to just
what kind of fig leaves these were which our first parents
found so convenient. Milton succeeds in individualizing this
too familiar story by mentioning "*Malabar* or *Decan,*" and
by giving one of the most detailed and freshly effective of
all his descriptions. We visualize the long arms of the tree,
the branches descending to earth and taking root again to
send up more trees, the delightful pillared shade high over-
arched where the Indian herdsman shelters himself from
the burning eastern heat and, through loopholes conveniently cut through thickets, watches his herds as they graze
at will. The passage is poetically the equal of the leviathan
passage of Book I; and it seems fresher—partly perhaps because so much less quoted.

In following the terrible depredations pursued by Sin and
Death fighting their way up through Chaos to fashion their
infernal causeway for the ruin of man, Milton employs a

[78] *P.L.*, Bk. IX, l. 1099ff.   [79] Genesis 3:7.

similar technique.[80] They are compared, it will be remembered, to two polar winds blowing adverse. Perhaps the most brilliant thing Milton does is to mention "*Cronian Sea*," which by the very word somehow succeeds in building up within the reader's mind an impression of classic traditionalism. No sooner is that impression made, however, than there comes the reference to "*Petsora* Eastward." Against a backdrop of the classics is projected a picture current and living, a picture of mountains of impassable ice blocking Englishmen's way to the long-sought northeast passage. Those who had read Hakluyt's and Purchas' heartbreaking descriptions of those insuperable hardships must have had a still deeper impression of the whole picture. By the time of *Paradise Lost* the fighting between Russians and Tartars had itself become almost traditional. And when Milton came to describe the devils awaiting in Hell the return of their great Chief from his conquest of man,[81] both he and his reader were fully aware of that tradition. The line, therefore, "as when the *Tartar* from his *Russian* Foe" would have promised nothing more than a well-known rivalry between two nations inimical to each other. As soon, however, as Astracan is mentioned in the next line, the temper of the passage changes; we get the feeling that a rather general allusion has been made specific indeed. The incident appears the more credible for being localized.[82] Even the "utmost *Indian* Isle *Taprobane*" of *Regained*,[83] referred to in Christ's vision, acquires special significance because, as we have seen,[84] the educated reader would immediately identify Taprobane with Sumatra.

For a last example of Milton's using his geographic de-

[80] *P.L.*, Bk. x, l. 289ff.   [81] *P.L.*, Bk. x, ll. 431-433.
[82] See previous discussion of these lines, pp. 53-54 *supra*.
In connection with the lines just below where Milton refers to the fighting between Persians and Turks in which all is left waste "beyond the Realme of *Aladule*," Gilbert (*op.cit.*, p. 14) calls attention to the fact that Heylyn records King Aladeule's resistance to the Turk.
[83] Bk. IV, l. 75.   [84] See p. 127 *supra*.

tails to reach an effect of definiteness and thus give his lines a sense of plausibleness, the famous comparison of Satan to a fleet engaged in East Indian trade[85] may be taken. One may say first that the great activities in the preceding years of the East India Company had made reference to the trade-route something of a commonplace. But the very mention not merely of the two tiny spice islands of Ternate and Tidore but of Bengala, itself so important in trade, raises the passage far above the commonplace. The cartographers and the voyagers had so presented those regions that the active associations with them lent a special sort of significance to their inclusion here. It is as if the passage, magnificent as the general picture is of a fleet beating its tortuous way through the vast Ethiopian Sea towards the Cape, took on meaning and credibility through the carefully chosen detail.

There is another poetic technique employed by Milton so closely allied to the foregoing that it is sometimes indistinguishable. But in this case the attempt is not so much the creation of an atmosphere of the traditional against which is placed a "modern" reference as it is the deliberate combination of an old name with a new, thus augmenting the associational value of the passage. It will be observed that in these instances the two allusions often complement each other in an interesting and subtle way. The overtones of the lines increase as they react upon each other. The interplay of image and association tends to make the passage fuller and richer. To take first a direct and undeveloped example, Milton compares Satan when haled before the judgment seat of Gabriel to,

> *Teneriff* or *Atlas* unremov'd:
> His stature reacht the Skie (Bk. iv, ll. 987-988).[86]

Because of the earth-bearing capacity of strong-shouldered

---

[85] *P.L.*, Bk. ii, ll. 636-642.
[86] These lines have been treated in another connection. See p. 80 *supra*.

Atlas, few figures of classical mythology were better known than he. And it was of course usual to associate him with the African mountain which either had been responsible for the myth in the first place or which had been accepted as its rationalization. On the other hand, there had been almost as many new associations with Tenerife, the sky-pointing peak of the Canaries which seamen delighted to tell tall tales about. Because the mountain rose directly out of the ocean, it gave approaching ships an impression of loftiness far in excess of the truth. In addition, there seems to have been something of a contest to see who could indulge in the most extravagant hyperbole. Heylyn,[87] among many, recorded this amazing height: "Tenariffe . . . is most remarkable for a Mountain of so great an height, that it may be seen 90 Leagues at Sea. . . . Some reckon it 15 miles high, . . . some advance it to 60 miles. . . . With truth enough most of our *Travellers* and *Geographers* hold it to be the highest in the whole world." Not merely was Milton aware of this reputation; he was aware that all those for whom he was writing were aware of it too. He could not have chosen an analogy which would create upon his reader's mind an impression of greater loftiness and stability.

A somewhat different effect is accomplished in another passage where a new name is deliberately joined with an old one. In the view which Michael unrolls to Adam the archangel reveals, *inter alia*,

> where
> The *Persian* in *Ecbatan* sate, or since
> In *Hispahan* (Bk. xi, ll. 392-394).

To the well-informed reader this would represent not merely a change in the site of Persia's capital but a vast change in time. Not only the cosmographies but the eastern histories had associated Ecbatan with early Persian history,[88] whereas

---

[87] *Cosmographie*, IV, 88.
[88] See Gilbert, *op.cit.*, p. 109. It was the capital only up to the time of the Greek conquest.

Hispahan was regularly associated with Shah Abbas the Great, a contemporary of Milton. Modern trade had made it famous, and a modern traveler had written that "the King that now raigneth makes most of his abode in Hispaan."[89] The reader is therefore carried from a period well before Christ down to the seventeenth century. The associations with Ecbatan are largely historical, with Hispahan, current and commercial; and the link between them is the Persian ruler.

An even more interesting example of Milton's adroit use of names, new and old, is to be found in his description of Satan's search for the animal into which he will creep to accomplish man's fall:

> Sea he had searcht and Land
> From *Eden* over *Pontus*, and the Poole
> *Maeotis*, up beyond the River *Ob*;
> Downward as farr Antartic; and in length
> West from *Orontes* to the Ocean barr'd
> At *Darien*, thence to the Land where flowes
> *Ganges* and *Indus* (Bk. ix, ll. 76-82).

From conventional Eden we are taken across the Black Sea (Pontus) and the Sea of Azov, the older associations with which are recalled by Milton's giving the classical name, "Poole (Palus) *Maeotis*." Next to these two comes the River Ob, an almost startlingly modern one since Milton's contemporaries would inevitably connect it with the English search for the Northeast Passage. The poet himself had read any number of stories about it in his Moscovian researches, and so had many of his readers. Naturally the river appeared prominently in *A Brief History*.[90] Orontes again is familiar and old ground as being the most important river in Syria; and then, at once, Darien. Why Darien? Clearly not for Keats' reason. Many conjectures have been offered, the most likely being the connection with

[89] Quoted from Purchas by Gilbert, *op.cit.*, p. 147.
[90] See previous discussion, pp. 51-52 *supra*.

Drake. However that may be, the poetic effect is to carry the reader into a world which, though distant, is immediate and real. The passage closes, as it began, with familiar and traditional allusions, to Ganges and Indus.

The two long passages in *Paradise Lost*, Book Eleven, and *Paradise Regained*, Book Three, have been analyzed in previous chapters. The chief point to notice here is the way Milton introduces the first of these, "City of old or modern Fame" (l. 386). A second point is that the poet has followed civilizations from early times down to the present, which he implies will decay just as the others. The very term "Sinaean" carries the mind back across the centuries, while "Cambalu" and "Cathaian" take us at least to Polo's time. "Agra" and "Lahor," on the other hand, belong in a different class. Here the associations, instead of being remote and romantic, were rather contemporary and commercial. Besides Heylyn, Milton might have found his information in Purchas, who has, for instance, a long and impressive account of Akbar's tomb near Agra.[91] Akbar, known as "the Great," died in 1605. Thus the "great *Mogul*" referred to lived into Milton's century. Furthermore, Purchas makes it clear that Agra is a thriving city at the present moment: "Agra is spacious, large, populous beyond measure, that you can hardly passe in the streets." Lahore receives similar important notice from Purchas, who records that it "is one of the greatest Cities of the East."[92] The references to the Russian Czar and to Moscow were, as has been seen, intimately bound up in Englishmen's minds with trade routes. They were, quite definitely, affairs of the moment. The places in Africa carry on the impression until we come to "*Sofala* thought *Ophir*," which again represents a deliberate attempt on the poet's part to remind us of a tradition as old as the Bible itself. "*Atlas* Mount" is similarly introduced

[91] Quoted by Gilbert, *op.cit.*, p. 13.
[92] Gilbert, *op.cit.*, pp. 168-169.

for its older associations because most of the surrounding allusions are of the present. America was thought of as being such a new affair that the tendency of every mention of it is, almost, to give the impression that poets are actually referring to the future. Ralegh's bitter experience had made Guiana an immediate concern, and there were doubtless many who still felt that El Dorado would yield her fabulous wealth. Possibly just because he felt these last names held associations so living in his countrymen's consciousness, Milton referred to the Spaniards as "*Geryons* Sons." This would at once swing the mind back to Virgil and Hercules.

In the *Paradise Regained* passage, where we have seen Milton's purpose was quite different, there is no such interesting commixture of new with the old. It is noteworthy, however, that even here, amidst allusions to ancient Nineveh, to Babylon, Persepolis, Ecbatana, and Caucasus, he puts, as if by way of reminder, "Candaor," which connoted something entirely separate from the rest. Gilbert[93] points out that "Candahar is a more modern name than some of those associated with it by Milton," and he quotes Purchas: "Candahar is a Citie of importance, which is frequented with Merchants of Turkie, Persia, and the parts of India." It should be further noted that Candahar was on one of the main trade-routes.

Much the same poetic effect is attained in Milton's list of wind-names.[94] In spite of these having all been taken from a contemporary geography,[95] the general impression they make is of Ptolemy and the classics. The poet was quite aware of that effect, and he therefore introduces right into the middle of them "Serraliona," which gives the modern touch. The very word is Spanish, and seventeenth-century mariners knew the region for the "black with thundrous Clouds" which Milton speaks of. Verity[96] quotes appositely

[93] *Op.cit.*, p. 72.
[95] Cf. *supra*, p. 123.
[94] *P.L.*, Bk. x, ll. 699-706.
[96] *Op.cit.*, p. 609.

from Hexham's *Mercator*: "Sierra Liona is . . . a very high Mount, the toppe whereof is continually hidde with snowe: from whence there comes fearefull noises, and great tempest." Sierra Leone was a regular stopover in East Indian trade. One last point should be noted. Milton chooses to put the winds with Italian names, "*Sirocco, and Libecchio*" at the end of his list.

The final example is in some ways the most characteristic of them all. It occurs in Book Five, when Eve goes forth to pluck the choicest fruit in Eden for Raphael's entertainment.

> Whatever Earth all-bearing Mother yeilds
> In *India* East or West, or middle shoare
> In *Pontus* or the *Punic* Coast, or where
> *Alcinous* reign'd, fruit of all kindes, in coate,
> Rough, or smooth rin'd, or bearded husk, or shell
> She gathers (ll. 338-343).

Scholars have quoted and cited a great variety of sources for the above passage. It has been shown[97] how Pliny referred to the "Filberds and Hazels" which "came out of Pontus," and to the cherry-tree's being introduced into Europe from Pontus. It has further been shown[98] how Strabo emphasizes the region's wild fruits, the pear, apple, and hazel. In addition, the African (Punic) coast was traditional for its fruit, especially for the fig.[99] The very mention of "*India* East or West" is significant since the former contained the older associations, the latter the new ones. And when we put this passage together with others in *Paradise Lost* which quite obviously refer to Indian fruits, as Gilbert[100] does, we are convinced that Milton has in mind, in addition to the classical descriptions, the modern ones as well. Above all writers Linschoten, whose book was called *Discours of Voyages into the Easte and West Indies*, furnished the most elaborate accounts. The extracts from his

[97] Verity, *op.cit.*, p. 489.   [98] Gilbert, *op.cit.*, pp. 236-237.
[99] Verity, *op.cit.*, p. 489.   [100] *Op.cit.*, pp. 153-155.

work which Professor Gilbert has so carefully selected illustrate convincingly what the poet has in mind. The remarkable qualities of the cocoanut as Linschoten gives them make it a likely fruit for a place in Paradise. He speaks, as Milton does, of the "huske or shell," every part of the fruit being useful for some purpose. In commenting on some lines allied with the ones quoted above, Gilbert mentions that doubtless the garden of Alcinous was in the back of Milton's mind. And in the passage with which we are immediately concerned we know that to be a fact since Alcinous is specifically mentioned. Here then is another instance where the poet ranges all the way from Homer to a traveler contemporary with himself. The lines become effective because the allusions are skillfully interwoven of the new and old, because associations with both are brought out or suggested, and because each is made to supplement the other.

CONCLUSION

IN ALL of the foregoing studies there are several basic factors which should be kept continually in mind. One is that from beginning to end Milton was apt to use materials which became an integral part of him in his unusually thorough training as a classical scholar. Because of that classical training, the famous River Ganges continues to do service as the eastern bounds of the world, from the period of the Third Latin Elegy (Milton was seventeen at the time) where the poet refers to "far-off borders, in the land of the Ganges,"[1] down to *Paradise Lost*[2] where we find him still using the river as the extreme eastern limit in spite of modern travelers' having pushed far out the bounds of the known world. He will persist in mentioning old names like "Syene," partly because they fitted the time about which he was writing, but partly also just because Pliny had used such terms. Strabo and Mela continued to function as "authorities" in this sense for the reason that he had early learned a deep respect for them.

The other point is that much of what these Ancients had recorded was perpetuated by Milton's favorites among the Moderns, such writers as Heylyn and Sandys and Fuller. This applies equally well to the Maps. After all, Ptolemy lies directly behind Ortelius and Mercator, behind Heylyn and Hexham. Sometimes this will amount with Milton to a localization of the old, such as the placing of Ophir. Certain materials because of their very nature will remain the stuff of poetry until the crack of doom. And so Milton goes on using Mount Niphates, Enna and Proserpina, Rhodope and Orpheus, the Hellespont and Xerxes, Pelorus, Libyan sands, and Ophiusa. Some things seem, then, to be perennial. Modern travelers neither proved nor disproved them. Babylon would always be magnificent and Persia would

[1] *Works*, I, 183. [2] Bk. IX, l. 82.

139

forever stand for oriental splendor. The Bible of course played in all this its determining role. It was the Word of God, and therefore continued in full force in spite of recent travelers' having cast serious doubt on some of its conclusions. Even here, however, the tendency was to confirm rather than disprove; and Sandys and Fuller are resorted to merely because they had contemporary versions of what had long been taken for granted.

Another factor, however, that must not be overlooked is that the poet in him sometimes made Milton retain the superstitions which he abjured so contemptuously in *A Brief History*. And so we have "the strange tales of Pliny," the remora, and the geese over Taurus. Closely allied is the reflection of romance materials. Every now and then one is reminded forcibly of Ariosto and Boiardo, of Tasso and Camões. Aspramont and Montalban, Trebisond and Biserta, Barca and Cyrene cannot help recalling pages in the great romances. And we are conscious too that Mombaza, Quiloa, and Melind appeared in the *Lusiads* as well as in the travelers. Milton, we may be sure, was aware of all this. He knew he could enrich his poetry still further by including the associations normally connected with these romantic materials.

In fact, herein lies the answer. It becomes progressively clear that Milton's whole objective was the true enrichment of that poetry. Without losing sight of what has previously been contended, that few poets sensed as he the value of continuing to fortify his lines with imagery based on geographical matter even when the new geographies had proved it to be wrong, we should observe how he still more characteristically makes the combination between the new and the old. Down to the end of his career, he was always capable, with his great and enduring admiration for the classics, of using some purely classical reference, however wrong, so long as it served his poetic purpose. So it was a

Conclusion

matter, not of discarding the old for the new, but of subjoining the new to the old and thus adding immeasurably to his treasure house of reference. It must be remembered also that the new geographies themselves did their part in perpetuating these old beliefs. Milton found, however, that he could use the new materials they furnished to intensify and objectify a passage by mention of one of their specific "modern" names—be it Norumbega, Astracan, or Petsora. This procedure makes the whole passage move forward in three-dimensional clarity. What he recalled from his own personal experience sometimes acted to the same purpose. One final factor we should not lose sight of is that both Milton and his readers enjoyed the proper names of geography for their sound alone, quite independent of their associational value. It is deplorable, however, when critics mistakenly deny that such passages have that associational value.

The most important impression of all that we bring away from a study of this kind is that *Paradise Lost*, with which inevitably we have been primarily occupied, contains, for a work basically classical and Biblical, an extraordinary amount of geographical material of the new kind. Actually, this amounts to saying that Milton, heir to the ages though he was, would not rest satisfied until he had used what the men of his own great century had contributed to the sum of knowledge.

BIBLIOGRAPHY

THIS bibliography lays no claim to being complete. It contains merely those items which I have found most useful in writing the book. For additional data the reader is referred to the appropriate sections in the Cambridge Bibliography of English Literature, especially to the section on travel books.

Where the place of publication is omitted, it will be understood to be London. The following abbreviations have been used:

CBEL	*Cambridge Bibliography of English Literature*
ELH	*Journal of English Literary History*
JEGP	*Journal of English and Germanic Philology*
MLN	*Modern Language Notes*
MLR	*Modern Language Review*
MP	*Modern Philology*
NQ	*Notes and Queries*
PMLA	*Publications of the Modern Language Association of America*
PQ	*Philological Quarterly*
RES	*Review of English Studies*
SP	*Studies in Philology*
TLS	*Times Literary Supplement* (London)

Abbot, George, *A Briefe Description of the Whole Worlde*, 1599.

Adrichomius, *Theatrum Terrae Sanctae*, Coloniae Agrippinae, 1593.

———, *Urbis, Hierosolimae Descriptio*, Coloniae Agrippinae, 1585. (Thomas Tymme's translation appeared in 1595.)

Barckley, Richard, *The Felicitie of Man*, 1598.

Blount, Thomas, *Glossographia*, 1656.

Bochart, Samuel, *Geographia Sacra*, 1681.

Breydenbach, *Peregrinatio in Terram Sanctam*, in civitate Moguntina, 1486.

Browne, Sir Thomas, *Works* (ed. Simon Wilkin), 4 vols., 1835-1836.

Bryant, J. A., Jr., "Milton and the Art of History," PQ, XXIX (1950), 15-30.

Bush, Douglas, *Mythology and the Renaissance Tradition in English Poetry*, Minneapolis, 1932.

Cavendish, W., *Two Comedies*, 1649.

Cawley, Robert R., *Milton's Literary Craftsmanship*, Princeton, 1941.

————, "Sir Thomas Browne and His Reading," PMLA, XLVIII (1933), 426-470.

————, *Unpathed Waters: Studies in the Influence of the Voyagers on Elizabethan Literature*, Princeton, 1940.

————, *The Voyagers and Elizabethan Drama*, Boston and London, 1938.

Clark, E. M., "Milton's Abyssinian Paradise" in the University of Texas *Studies in English*, XXIX (1950), 129-150.

Cook, A. S., "Two Notes on Milton," MLR, II (1906-1907), 121-128.

Cooper, Lane, "The Abyssinian Paradise in Coleridge and Milton," MP, III (1906), 327-332.

Davity, Pierre, *The Estates, Empires, and Principallities of the World* (trans. E. Grimstone), 1615.

Diodorus Siculus, *The History* (trans. Henry Cogan), 1653.

————, *The Historical Library*, 2 vols., 1814.

Draper, J. W., "Milton's Ormus," MLR, XX (1925), 323-327.

Early Voyages and Travels to Russia and Persia, 2 vols., vols. 72 and 73, 1886.

Eden, Richard, and Willes, Richard, *The History of Travayle in the West and East Indies*, 1577.

First Three English Books on America (ed. Arber), Birmingham, 1885.

Fletcher, Giles, Sr., *The History of Russia*, 1656.

————, *Of the Russe Common Wealth*, 1591.

Fletcher, Giles and Phineas, *Poetical Works*, 2 vols., Cambridge University Press, 1908-1909.

Foster, Sir William, *England's Quest of Eastern Trade*, 1933.

————, "Milton and India," TLS, April 6, 1933, p. 248.

Fuller, Thomas, *The History of the Holy Warre*, Cambridge, 1639.

————, *A Pisgah-Sight of Palestine*, 1650.

Gerard, John, *Herball*, 1597.

Gilbert, A. H., *A Geographical Dictionary of Milton*, Yale University Press, 1919.

————, "Milton's China," MLN, XXVI (1911), 199-200.

————, "Pierre Davity: His Geography and its Use by Milton," *Geographical Review*, VII (1919), 322-336.

Giovio, Paulo, *Moschovia*, Basil, 1561.

Gordon, D. J., "Two Milton Notes," RES, XVIII (1942), 318-319.

Greaves, John, *Pyramidographia: or, a description of the pyramids in Aegypt*, 1646.

Bibliography

Hakluyt, Richard, *The Principal Navigations Voyages Traffiques and Discoveries of the English Nation*, 12 vols., Glasgow, 1903-1905.

Hamel, J., *England and Russia*, 1854.

Hanford, J. H., *John Milton, Englishman*, New York, 1949.

———, "Milton and the Art of War," SP, XVIII (1921), 232-266.

Herberstein, Siegmund von, *Rerum Muscoviticarum Commentarii*, Vienna, 1549.

Heylyn, Peter, *Cosmographie in four bookes, containing the chorographie and historie of the whole world*, 1652.

———, *Cosmographie in Four Books*, 1670.

———, *Microcosmos: A Little Description of the Great World*, Oxford, 1636.

Josephus, *Antiquitates Judaicae*, Venetiis, 1480 (?).

Knolles, Richard, *The Generall Historie of the Turkes*, 1603.

Leo Africanus, *A Geographical Historie of Africa* (trans. John Pory), 1600.

———, *The History and Description of Africa*, 3 vols., Hakluyt Society, 1896.

Linschoten, Jan Huyghen van, *His Discours of Voyages into the Easte and West Indies*, 1598.

Lockwood, L. E., "A Note on Milton's Geography," MLN, XXI (1906), 86.

Lodge, Thomas, *Complete Works*, 4 vols., Hunterian Club [Glasgow], 1883.

McColley, Grant, *Paradise Lost*, Chicago, 1940.

Marshall, E. H., "Paradise Lost, I, 587," NQ, Ser. VII, no. xii (1891), 456-457.

Martyr, Peter, *De Orbe Novo*, 2 vols., New York and London, 1912.

Mela, Pomponius, *The Worke of P.M. The Cosmographer, concerninge the Situation of the world* (trans. Arthur Golding), 1585.

Mercator, Gerardus, *Atlas; or, a Geographicke Description of the World* (ed. Henry Hexham), Amsterdam, 1636.

Milton, John, *A Brief History of Moscovia* (ed. D. S. Mirsky), 1929.

———, *Comus and Lycidas* (ed. A. W. Verity), Cambridge, 1898.

———, *English Poems by John Milton* (ed. R. C. Browne), 2 vols., Oxford: Clarendon Press, 1902-1906.

———, *Facsimile of the Manuscript of Milton's Minor Poems* (W. A. Wright), Cambridge, 1899.

———, *The Latin Poems* (ed. and trans. Walter MacKellar), Yale University Press, 1930.

———, *Ode on the Morning of Christ's Nativity, L'Allegro, Il Penseroso, and Lycidas* (ed. A. W. Verity), Cambridge, 1931.

———, *Of Reformation* (ed. W. T. Hale), *Yale Studies in English*, vol. LIV, New Haven, 1916.

———, *Paradise Lost* (ed. A. W. Verity), Cambridge, 1910.

———, *Paradise Regained* (ed. C. S. Jerram), 1877.

———, *Paradise Regained* (ed. E. H. Blakeney), 1932.

———, *Paradise Regained, the Minor Poems and Samson Agonistes* (ed. M. Y. Hughes), New York, 1937.

———, *Poetical Works* (ed. H. J. Todd), 7 vols., 1809.

———, *Poetical Works* (E. Hawkins), 4 vols., Oxford and London, 1824.

———, *Poetical Works* (ed. D. Masson), 3 vols., New York and London, 1894.

———, *Poetical Works* (ed. H. C. Beeching), Oxford University Press, New York, 1935.

———, *Prose Works* (ed. J. A. St. John), 5 vols. (Bohn's Standard Library), 1848-1853.

———, *Samson Agonistes* (ed. A. W. Verity), Cambridge, 1932.

———, *Works*, 18 vols., New York, 1931-1938.

Moore, Andrew, *A Compendious History of the Turks*, 1660.

Mutschmann, Heinrich, *Milton in Russland*, Dorpat, 1924.

———, "Studies Concerning the Origin of 'Paradise Lost,'" Dorpat, 1924.

Nicolson, Marjorie, "Milton's Hell and the Phlegraean Fields," *University of Toronto Quarterly*, VII, 500-513 (July, 1938).

Nordenskiöld, A. E., *Facsimile-Atlas to the Early History of Cartography*, Stockholm, 1889.

North, George, *The Description of Swedland, Gotland, and Finland . . . chieflye out of Sebastian Mounster*, 1561.

Notes Upon Russia, 2 vols., Hakluyt Soc., vols. 10 and 12, 1851-1852.

Olaus Magnus, *A Compendious History of the Goths, Swedes, and Vandals, and Other Northern Nations*, 1658.

"Ormuz and Amurath," TLS, March 30, 1933, pp. 205-206.

Ortelius, Abraham, *Theatrum Orbis Terrarum*, Antwerp, 1612.

Bibliography

Osgood, C. G., *The Classical Mythology of Milton's English Poems,* New York, 1900.

Parks, G. B., "The Occasion of Milton's *Moscovia,*" SP, XL (1943), 399-404.

Pliny the Elder, *Natural History* (trans. J. Bostock and H. T. Riley), 6 vols., Bohn's Classical Library, 1855-1857.

Polo, Marco, *The Book of Ser Marco Polo* (ed. H. Yule), 2 vols., 1903.

Pope, E. M., *Paradise Regained,* Johns Hopkins Press, 1947.

Purchas, Samuel, *His Pilgrimage; or Relations of the World and the Religions Observed in all Ages,* 1613.

———, *Hakluytus Posthumus or Purchas his Pilgrimes,* 4 vols., 1625.

———, *Hakluytus Posthumus or Purchas His Pilgrimes,* 20 vols., Glasgow, 1905-1907.

Ralegh, Sir Walter, *The Discoverie of the large, rich and bewtiful Empyre of Guiana,* 1596.

———, *Works,* 8 vols., Oxford University Press, 1829.

Russia at the Close of the Sixteenth Century, Hakluyt Soc., vol. XX, 1856.

Russia Seu Moscovia Itemque Tartaria Commentario Topographico Atque Politico Illustratae. Lug[duni] Batavorum, 1630. (The so-called "Elzevir" *Russia.*)

Sandys, George, *A Relation of a Journey begun An. Dom. 1610,* 1621.

Seaton, Ethel, "Marlowe's Map," *Essays and Studies by Members of the English Association* (vol. X, 13-35), Oxford University Press, 1924.

Sir Thomas Smithes Voiage and Entertainment in Rushia, 1605.

Speed, John, *A Prospect of the Most Famous Parts of the World,* 1668.

Strabo, *Geography,* 8 vols., Loeb Classical Library, 1917—.

Sugden, E. H., *A Topographical Dictionary to the Works of Shakespeare and his Fellow Dramatists,* Manchester, 1925.

Taylor, G. C., *Milton's Use of Du Bartas,* Cambridge, Mass., 1934.

Taylor, Isaac, "Milton's Estotiland," NQ, Ser. VIII, no. vii (1895), 421, 461-462.

Thompson, E. N. S., "Milton's Knowledge of Geography," SP, XVI, 148-171.

Three Voyages by the North-East Towards Cathay and China, Hakluyt Soc., vol. XIII, 1853.

Bibliography

Tihany, L. C., "Milton's 'Brief History of Moscovia,'" PQ, XIII (1934), 305-306.

Whiting, G. W., *Milton's Literary Milieu*, University of North Carolina Press, 1939.

——, "Milton's 'Taprobane,'" RES, XIII (1937), 209-212.

INDEX

Abbana, 110

Abbot, George, 45

Abyssinia (Ethiopia), 15, 16, 16n, 17, 66, 67-70, 89; princes guarded, 69-70, 89, 129

Accaron, 105, 119

Adam, 9, 24, 81, 83, 98, 130, 133

Adams, Clement, 47, 60, 62; Milton followed his narrative closely, 60

Adiabene, 27, 27n, 28, 36, 36n

Adonis, 73

Adrichomius, 110

Aelian, 35n

Aetna, Mount, 75, 75n, 76; site of Hell-mouth, 75

Africa, 3, 15ff, 23, 68, 68n, 70, 72, 76, 93, 95, 114, 133, 135, 137

Agra, 13, 14, 98, 135; populous, 135

Akbar, 135

Aladeule, King, 131n

Algiers, 17, 18, 19, 93, 114; pirates, 126

Almansor, 17, 18, 91

Alp, 73, 127

Amalthea, 72, 113, 117-118

Amanuenses, 22, 23, 26, 47, 64, 70, 97, 100

Amara, Mount, 16, 69-70, 89, 97, 129

Amazonian targe, 98

Amboyna, 84, 85n; slaughter of English at, 84

America, 4, 11, 19, 90, 94, 126n, 136

Ammianus Marcellinus, 35n, 77

Andes, 21

Angola, 16, 17, 17n

Antioch, luxurious kings of, 33, 34, 34n, 39

Anubis, 66, 104

Aonian Mount, 73

Arabia, 25, 27, 27n, 66, 71-72, 79, 101; Milton kept old conceptions about, 71; off-shore fragrance, 71-72, 114, 115n, 122, 125; three-fold division, 71; people thieves, 71, 71n

Arachosia, 26, 27, 35, 37

Araxes, River, 27, 27n, 30n

Archangel, 48

Arecca betula, 86, 126

Ariosto, 14n, 51n, 95, 140

Aristotle, 65

Armenia, 33

Arsaces, King, 33, 33n, 34; founder of the Parthian family, 33

Artaxata, 32

Arthur, King, 53; conquers "as far as Russia," 44n

Arzina, 60

Ascalon, 105, 105n, 119

Aspramont, 95, 140

Assyria, 25, 26, 27n, 28, 36, 122

Astracan, 49, 52, 53, 54, 54n, 55, 58, 116, 131, 141

Atabalipa, 19, 20, 20n; spelling of, 20, 20n, 96, 102n

Athens, 125, 128

Atlas, Mount, 17, 17n, 80, 114, 132, 133, 135-136

Atropatia, 30n, 36, 37

Augustine, 111

Azotus, 105, 112n, 119

Babel, Tower of, 29, 121

Babylon, 25, 26, 27, 28, 29, 30, 32, 33, 38, 39, 41, 121, 122, 136, 139; accounted one of the world's nine wonders, 29

Bactria, 12

Balsara, 26, 27, 30, 32n, 33, 36, 36n

Banda, 84n

Bannister-Ducket voyage, 54

Barbary, 17, 19n

Barckley, Richard, 45

Barents, William, 43, 47

Index

Bayona's hold, 94
Beaumont and Fletcher, 53
Beelzebub, 61, 64n
Belus, 104n
Bengala, 69, 95, 95n, 132
Blaeu, 3, 124
Blount, Thomas, 107n
Bochart, Samuel, 76n, 110
Boghar, 48
Boiardo, 95, 140
Bowes, Jerome, 44
Breydenbach, 101, 110
Browne, R. C., 34, 125
Browne, Sir Thomas, 76n, 81-82, 82n
Bryant, J. A., Jr., 85n
Burrough, Stephen, 44, 51
Bush, Douglas, 108n
Byzantium, 15n

Cabot, Sebastian, 57n
Cairo, 95, 122; sometimes identified with Memphis, 103n, 122
Calabria, 114
Cambaluc, 9, 12, 22, 48, 91, 135; thought by some to be distinct from Pekin, 13, 13n, 83
Cambridge University, 65
Camões, 16n, 95n, 140
Canada, 58n, 88, 90
Canaries, 75, 79, 133
Candaor, 26, 27, 27n, 35, 96, 136
Cape of Good Hope, 68, 69, 71, 132
Capreae, 119
Carthaginian, methods of fighting, 40
Cartwright, 15n
Caspian Sea, 25, 35, 36, 36n, 37, 48, 49, 53, 54; C. tiger, 73; storminess, 49, 49n, 50
Cassius, Mount, 106
Cathay, 9, 12, 44, 48, 56, 57, 57n, 58n, 83, 85, 88, 91, 95, 101, 135; riches, 57, 58n; thought by some to be distinct from China, 13, 83, 101

Caucasus, 35, 73, 136
Cavendish, Thomas, 80n
Cawley, R. R., 40n, 45n, 50n, 55n, 58n, 60n, 71n, 75n, 76n, 78n, 80n, 81n, 82n, 91n, 95n, 101n, 104n, 116n
Ceylon, 127
Chaldaea, 77, 93
Chancellor, Richard, 44, 47, 56, 60, 62, 63n; begins negotiations with Ivan, 44
Charlemagne, 125
Charybdis, 107-108, 108n
Chaucer, 53
Chersonese, 14, 23, 76, 91n
China, 3, 12, 13, 13n, 48, 83, 91, 91n, 101, 122, 125
Chinese, 91, 122; sail-wagons, 91, 91n, 126-127
Choaspes (Eulaeus), River, 27, 31, 31n, 39-40; the drink of none but kings, 31, 40, 120-121
Christ, 24, 25, 38, 40, 87, 105, 131, 134; advised by Satan to get control of the Parthian empire, 38; condemns warfare, 40
Cimmerian, 73
Clark, E. M., 70n
Claudian, 108n
Congo, 16, 17n, 126; natives reject Christianity, 101n
Cook, A. S., 94, 113
Cooper, Lane, 70
Coryat, Thomas, 79
Cronian Sea, 57, 131
Ctesiphon, 27, 30, 32, 32n, 33, 34, 36, 38, 39; Parthian king gathers his host in, 34
Cusco, 19, 20, 20n, 21, 96
Cyrus, 25, 29, 34; sets Israelites free, 29
Czar, 15n, 42, 42n, 44, 44n, 49, 50, 64n, 135; his tyranny, 74, 74n

Dagon, 105, 105n, 111, 112, 112n, 119

Index

Damasco, 108n, 110
Damiata, 106
Danube River, 91, 95
Darien, 4, 134
Davity, Pierre, 5, 16n, 84, 84n, 91n, 97
Dead Sea, 106, 115n, 118; apples, 118
Deccan, 4, 98, 130
Dee, Dr. John, 56n; refuses Czar's offer, 44
Delos, 126
Diodorus Siculus, 5, 21n, 28, 30n, 37, 71, 72, 106, 106n, 107n, 108n, 111, 115n, 117, 118, 122
Drake, Sir Francis, 135
Draper, J. W., 79
Du Bartas, 51n
Dvina, River, 48

East India Company, 84-85, 84n, 132
Ecbatana, 14, 15, 15n, 30, 31, 32, 36, 38, 39, 93, 100, 133, 133n, 134, 136; its magnificence, 30
Eden, Richard, 52n, 56, 80; his account of Russia, 43
Eden, 51, 129, 134, 137
Egypt, 4, 17, 65, 81, 82, 102, 122; gods, 66, 66n; pyramids, 66-67, 102n, 103, 119-120; rain scarce in, 66, 66n, 104, 104n; religion, 104; tyranny, 74
El Dorado (Manoa), 20, 20n, 21, 136
Emathian, see under Macedon
Enna, 108, 139; fair field of, 6, 113
Equator, passing through Mount Amara, 70, 89
Ercoco, 15, 16, 16n, 100
Escalante, Barnardine of, 91n
Estotiland, 90, 90n, 94, 130; extreme cold, 90
Ethiopia, see under Abyssinia
Ethiopian Sea, 132; east or west of Africa?, 67-68, 93, 95

Etruria, sorcerers, 81, 116
Euphrates River, 25, 27n, 33, 121
Eve, 69
Evelyn, John, 78

Fez, 17, 18, 18n, 114
Fiesole, 127, 128
Figtree passage, 115n, 130; probably not from travelers at all, 98-99
Finch, Richard, 59
Fletcher, Giles Sr., 5, 29n, 43, 43n, 45, 47, 50, 52, 54, 55, 74n, 80-81, 85, 88; describes favorable side of Russia, 45-46; his book suppressed, 43n, 46; Milton admired his account of Russia, 43
Fletcher, Phineas, 35n, 53, 54, 55
Florence, 128
Fontarabbia, 125
Fortunate Islands, 74-75, 75n, 120
Foster, Sir William, 42n, 78n, 127
Fritsch, Charles, 29n
Fuller, Thomas, 5, 7, 29n, 66n, 74n, 82, 82n, 103n, 104n, 107n, 108n, 109-113, 115, 117, 122, 123, 139, 140; *Pisgah-Sight*, probable influence of, 109 ff, engravings in, 109, 111, 112-113

Ganges, River, 90, 121, 125, 134, 135, 139
Gath, 110
Gaza, 103, 105, 105n, 110, 118
Georgia, 36n, 99
Gerard, John, probable influence on figtree passage, 99, 115n
Geryon, 20, 21, 21n, 136
Gilbert, A. H., vii, 13n, 14n, 15, 18, 20n, 26n, 28, 35, 36n, 48, 54, 59n, 66, 67n, 76, 77, 78n, 84n, 90n, 91n, 95, 97, 99, 100, 101, 110n, 111, 113, 114, 119n, 121n, 122, 126n, 131n, 133n, 135n, 136, 137, 138
Gill, Alexander Sr., 65

Index

Giovio, Paolo, 44-45; his *Moschovia*, 43

Golgotha, 87, 105

Goodwin sands, 76

Gordon, D. J., 14n

Gourdon, William, 58, 59, 86, 100

Greaves, John, Oxford professor of Astronomy, 67, 67n

Greece, 32, 65, 66, 102, 103, 107

Griffith, Matthew, 124n

Guiana, 20, 20n, 21, 21n, 126, 136; interest of English in, 21n, 136

Hakluyt, Richard, 4, 19n, 20n, 30n, 42, 43, 44n, 46, 47, 51n, 52, 54, 55, 56n, 57n, 58n, 59n, 62n, 63n, 64n, 75, 78, 85, 95n, 99, 102n, 116, 116n, 117, 121, 122, 131; used extensively in writing of *History of Moscovia*, 47, 49, 49n, 50n, 64

Hall, Joseph, Bishop, 87n, 114

Hamel, J., 43n

Hanford, J. H., 35n, 40

Haran, 77

Hecatompylos, 15, 31, 33n, 39; and her hundred gates, 31

Hecla, Mount, site of Hell-mouth, 75

Heimbach, Peter, 21, 123-124

Hellespont, 107, 107n, 118, 139

Hell-mouth, 121

Herberstein, Sigismundus, 43

Herodotus, 31, 37, 107, 118, 121

Hesiod, 111

Hesperean, 99

Hesperides, a place, not people, 92

Hexham's Mercator, 68, 91, 93-96, 117, 137, 139; spelling often diverges from Milton's, 96, 125

Heylyn, Peter, 5, 7, 11, 12, 13, 14, 15, 16, 17, 18, 19, 20, 21, 22, 23, 24, 26, 27, 28, 29, 30, 31, 32, 33, 34, 35, 36, 37, 38, 39, 43n, 46, 46n, 51n, 52, 57, 68, 68n, 69, 70, 71, 72, 76, 77, 78, 79, 79n, 80, 81, 88, 89, 89n, 90, 91, 91n, 92, 93, 94, 95, 96, 97, 98, 100, 114, 115, 116, 117, 120, 121, 122, 131n, 133, 135, 139; catalytic agent, 37; combination of historical with geographic, 26, 28, 34, 37, 88, 96; *Cosmographie* kind of book useful to Milton, 21-22, 23, 46, 88-89; emphasis on decayed glory of older civilizations, 22, 30n, 32, 39; great extent of his influence on Milton, 6, 11 ff., 24 ff., 37, 88-93; *Microcosmos*, 11n, 13n, 14n, 68n, 78n, 88n, 92, 96n; on Cathay and China, 13; popularity of his work, 88, 88n, 93; Russians, his opinion of, 89n; spellings like Milton's, 18 ff., 28n, 29n, 37, 89, 90, 91, 91n, 94

Hidaspis, River, 90, 91, 96, 121

Hinnom, Valley of, 105, 119

Hispahan, 14, 15, 15n, 31n, 33n, 100, 133, 134

Holland, Philemon, 36n

Holy Land, 4, 102, 105, 110

Homer, 108, 123, 138

Horton, 65

Hughes, M. Y., 26n, 35n, 36n

Hyrcania, 26, 35, 36, 37

Iberia, 35, 36, 100; dark dales, 35-36, 99

Iceland, 73, 75

Imaus, Mount, 90, 91, 125

Incas, 20

India (east), 3, 13, 14, 44, 68, 76, 78, 79, 88, 90, 116, 121, 126, 127, 131, 132, 136, 137; Milton and, 60n, 66

Indians (east), 4, 86, 98, 130

Indians (west), 101, 101n, 126; dullest of mortals, 101n; Spanish tyranny over, 74; sun-worship by, 101, 101n, 126

Indus River, 25, 90, 121, 125, 134, 135

Index

Isis, 66, 104, 104n
Israel, 28, 37
Italy, 73, 102

Jansen (Jansson), 3, 123-124
Jenghis Khan, 91
Jenkinson, Anthony, 43n, 44, 49, 50n, 54, 56
'Jerram, C. S., 26n
Jerusalem, 29, 29n, 38
Jonah, Book of, 28
Jonas, Arngrimus, defense of Iceland, 75
Jonson, Ben, 67n, 91n
Jordan, derivation of name, 108, 108n
Josephus, 118, 120; *Antiquitates*, 110
Juvenal, 73

Khan, 9, 12, 83, 95
King James, 44
Knolles, Richard, *Historie of the Turkes*, 128, 128n

Ladon, 73
Lahore, 13, 98, 135
Lapland, 60; witches, 50, 50n, 80, 81, 116
Leo Africanus, 16, 17n, 18, 18n, 19, 23, 67, 86, 100, 114, 126
Libya, 17, 73, 139
Linschoten, 98, 98n, 114n-115n, 137, 138
Lockwood, L. E., 113, 113n, 118, 125
Locusts, 66n
Lodge, Thomas, 72n
Logan, Josias, 59
London, 73
Lucan, 76n, 107n
Lydia, 73

Macedon, 26, 32, 32n, 40
MacKellar, Walter, 73n
Maeotis (Sea of Azof), 51, 134

Magellan, Straits of, 90
Mahomet, 128; tomb at Medina, not Mecca, 78, 78n
Malabar, 4, 98, 130
Malacca, 76
Mandelslo, 79
Mandeville, Sir John, 102, 120
Maps, 11, 68, 69, 123-126
Margiana, 35, 37
Marlowe, Christopher, 49n, 68, 69, 72, 78
Marshall, E. H., 125
Martial, 65, 67
Martyr, Peter, 19n
Masson, David, 10, 72, 74n, 125
McColley, Grant, 70n, 97n
Mecca, 77, 78
Medes, 14
Media, 36, 37
Medina, tomb of Mahomet at, 78, 78n
Mela, Pomponius, 5, 92, 139
Melinde, 15, 16, 98, 140
Memphis, 67, 95, 103, 103n, 122
Mendoza, 91
Mercator, 68n, 72n, 82, 91n, 93-96, 139
Mesopotamia, 27n, 77
Mexico, 9, 19, 20; richness of, 19
Michael, 9, 12, 24, 48, 81, 83, 133
Milton, John, accuracy of geographic allusions, 5, 10, 22, 71-72, 93, 123, 124, 125, 126; *Animadversions*, 87n, 104, 113-114; *Apology*, 71, 87n; appropriateness of geographic allusions, 6; archaizing material, 73, 121; *Areopagitica*, 57n-58n, 65, 88; blindness, 21, 26, 64, 69, 93, 97, 109n, 116; *Brief History of Moscovia*, 3, 5, 6, 7, 40, 42, 42n, 43, 44, 46, 47, 48, 49, 50, 51, 52, 54, 55, 58, 58n, 59, 59n, 60-63, 64n, 74, 81, 85, 86, 87, 97, 100, 116, 117, 122, 126, 134, 140, date of the work, 85, 85n, his reason for writing it,

Index

42, 42n, preparations for writing, 46, 85, 134, stepping stone between early and late allusions, 7, 64, 81, 85-86; broadmindedness, 11n; classics and Bible, under spell of, 4, 7, 25, 28, 29, 38, 65-66, 69, 75, 76, 77, 87, 93, 103, 107, 109, 110, 110n, 111, 117, 119, 121, 122, 124, 127, 136, 139, 140, 141; combining historic with geographic, 27-28, 37, 96, 109; combining new and old geographic material, 7, 26, 83, 116 ff; *Commonplace Book*, 17n, 18n, 42n, 74, 86, 97, 101n, 114, 126; *Comus*, 65, 113, 116; conception of whale partly from voyagers, 50n-51n, 122; *De Doctrina Christiana*, 87-88; divorce, attitude towards, 42, 42n; *Doctrine and Discipline*, 67n, 101; eagerness to learn about foreign countries, 44-45, 48, 84-85, 87, 126; *Eikonoklastes*, 19, 74, 77, 129; emphasis on decay of civilizations, 10, 22, 24, 25, 38-39, 40, 135; enrichment of poetry, 83, 88, 96, 103n, 117, 118, 132, 140, 141; First *Defense*, 45, 73, 124; fruit of that forbidden tree, 24; Fuller, shared some of his attitudes towards geography, 109-113; geography, his theory of, 3, 88, 123; growth of geographic knowledge, 84-85 ff.; Hakluyt, incidental references to, 102n; Hexham, not used by M. so extensively as Heylyn, 93-94; Heylyn suited his purposes, 21-23, 26, 28, 37, 88-93, but sometimes differed with him, 92-93; *History of Britain*, 44n, 87, voyaging figures in, 87, 87n; *Il Penseroso*, 117; immediacy of allusions, 127; impressed with the evanescence of human glory, 10, 22, 24, 25, 38-39, 67; indi-

vidualization, 39-40, 40n; *In Quintum Novembris*, 65, 75, 81, 116; insistence on improving the original, 23, 54; integrates geography with story, 25, 37; interest in all forms of religion, 101; knowledge of English trade, 42n, 85; knowledge of history, 10, 25, 29, 32, 33; *L'Allegro*, 65; Lapland witches, 81; "leviathan," 50n-51n; Logic, work on, 88; *Lycidas*, 65, 94, 113; maps and atlases, his interest in, 3, 21, 26, 37, 69, 70, 72, 113n, 123-126, 139; military affairs, interest in, 40; mountains, likes to describe, 127; nationalism, 44, 44n, 55-56, 60-63, 86-87; Nativity Ode, 66, 103, 104; Northeast Passage, his interest in, 57 ff., 126, 131; objectification, 54, 58, 129 ff., 141; official position, 5, 23, 42, 64, 84, 85n, 126n, 129; often follows Heylyn's spelling, 18, 19, 37; opposed to arms, 40; Ortelius, regarded by M. as an authority, 113; pagan divinities, 102n, 104, 104n, 105, 106, 110, 111-113, 113n; *Paradise Lost*, 4, 5, 6, 9, 9n, 11n, 12, 13, 14, 15, 15n, 16, 17, 19, 20, 22, 23, 24, 30, 31n, 32n, 37, 45, 47, 49, 50, 50n, 51, 51n, 53, 57, 58n, 61, 62, 63, 64, 67, 68, 69, 70n, 71, 71n, 72, 74, 75, 77, 79, 80, 81, 82, 83, 86, 87, 89, 90, 91, 92, 93, 95, 96, 97, 98, 99, 100, 101, 103, 104, 105, 106, 107, 108, 109, 110, 111, 112, 113, 114, 115, 116, 117, 118, 119, 120, 121, 122, 123, 124, 125, 126, 127, 128, 129, 130, 131, 132, 133, 134, 135, 136, 137, 139, 141; *Paradise Regained*, 24 ff., 26n, 71, 89, 91n, 92, 99, 119, 123, 125, 127, 128, 131, 135, 136; personal experience, 127, 128, 141; poetic adaptation of

Index

geography, 9 ff., 26, 31, 40, 48, 52, 55, 57-59, 60-63, 69, 73, 83, 86, 88, 106, 107, 125-126, 130, 134-135, 138, 140: poetic progress, 25; preference for eye-witnesses, 47, 78n, 85, 97, 109; probably identifies Pekin with Cambaluc, China with Cathay, 13, 48, 101; *Prolusions*, 68n, 74, 75, 75n, 81 81n, 88, 101n, 122n, 126n, 129n; proper names, his fondness for, 10, 23, 24, 25, 39, 141; *Pro Se Defensio*, 67; Purchas, used him often for incidental references, 97, 99; pyramids, symbols of man's vanity, 67, 103-104; *Ready and Easy Way*, 65n; *Reason of Church Government*, 74; refrains from modernizing, 74 ff., 78; romances, his use of, 140; Russia, his interest in, 3, 6, 7, 42 ff., 73-74, 85; *Samson Agonistes*, 103, 103n, 110-111, 118, 123; Sandys, takes from him incidental references, 102-103; Second *Defense*, 101n; study of geography profitable, 3, 88; super-stitions, 88, 140; thanks Heim-bach, 21; three stages in use of geographic materials, 4 ff.; took care with spelling, 18-19, 100; traditionalism, 65 ff.; trip to Italy, 75, 103, 127, 128; Turks, low opinion of, 128-129, 129n; tutor-ing, 84; use of the best authori-ties, 25-26, 69, 72, 85, 113, 125; use of many books, 23; used modern travelers to rejuvenate old material, 66-67, 103, 106, 107, 113, 113n, 117, 118, 119, 120, 121, 123; using words near to original form, 15n, 18, 18n, 19, 64n; Willoughby, Sir Hugh, his interest in, 56, 60-62

Mogul, 13, 14, 135

Moloch, 103, 103n, 105, 105n, 111, 118, 119
Moluccas, 84n, 95
Mombaza, 15, 16, 98, 140
Montaigne, 35
Montezuma, 9, 18n, 19, 19n, 22, 96
Moore, Andrew, 128
Morocco, 17, 18, 18n, 19, 114
Moscow, 15n, 44, 49, 52, 135; burn-ing of, 52; Tartars claim posses-sion of, 55
Mozambique, 71, 72
Munster, Sebastian, 43
Muscovy Company, 43, 46, 56
Mutschmann, H., 60n

Namancos, 94
Nebuchadnezzar, 29, 29n, 32, 38; leads Jews into captivity, 29
Negus, 15, 100, 114
New England, 94
Nicator, Seleucus, 32
Nicolson, Marjorie, 75n, 108n
Niger, 17, 17n, 114
Nile, 17n, 66, 69, 104; Egypt's east-ern boundary, 82; monster-spawn-ing mud, 82; seven mouths, 81-82; source, 126
Nimrod, 28, 121
Nineveh, 28, 28n, 30, 38, 39, 66, 96, 115n, 126, 136
Ninus, 28, 28n
Niphates, Mount, 139
Nisibis, 32
Nordenskiöld, 68n, 72n
Northeast Passage, 43-44, 60-63, 86, 88, 126, 131, 134; regarded as an *English* project, 44, 44n, 56 ff., 86; terrible cold, 57, 58, 59
Norumbega, 47, 90, 94, 130, 141
Norway, 50n, 51n, 63n, 122; pine, 95
Nova Zembla, 58, 59
Numidian poets, 86, 126
Nyseian Isle, 113, 125

155

Index

Ob, River, 51, 51n, 52, 57, 134
Olaus Magnus, 5; probable source of sailors' mooring by whale's side, 51n, 122
Olympus, Mount, 73
Ophir, 15, 16, 97, 98, 120, 135, 139
Ophiusa, 76, 139
Oreb, 101
Orion, 73
Orkney Islands, 73
Ormus, 78, 78n, 79, 79n, 83n, 94; great wealth, 79, 92, 94; importance in trade, 78; proverb connected with, 79, 79n
Orontes, 134
Ortelius, Abraham, 15, 16, 16n, 19n, 20n, 26, 36n, 68n, 69, 72n, 82, 91, 91n, 94, 98, 98n, 99, 100, 106n, 108, 113-114, 115n, 117, 120, 123, 125, 139
Osgood, C. G., 21n, 82n
Osiris, 66, 104, 104n
Ovid, 65, 76n, 82, 108n, 115, 126
Oxus, 12, 12n, 89, 89n, 125

Pacorus, King, 27, 33
Palestine, 29n, 102, 104, 105, 118
Pandemonium, 60, 67, 82, 123, 127
Paneas, 108n, 110n, 121-122
Parks, G. B., 47n
Parthians, 25, 26, 27, 31, 32, 33, 34, 34n, 37, 38, 39; great power of their empire, 38, 41; insolence of princes, 34; methods of fighting, 34-35, 39, 40, 116
Pechora, 57, 58, 59, 86, 100, 131, 141
Pekin, 12, 13, 48, 83
Pelorus, 75, 139
Persepolis, 30, 30n, 38, 136; splendors, 30
Persia, 14, 15n, 26, 27, 30n, 32, 33n, 49, 54, 73, 79, 80, 94, 133, 134, 136; splendor, 122, 139-140
Persians, 14, 30, 31, 34, 40, 79, 100, 121, 131n, 133, 133n

Peru, 19, 20; great wealth, 20n, 21
Pet and Jackman voyage, 56, 58, 100
Pharphar, 110
Phillips brothers, 65, 84
Phlegraean Fields, and Milton's Hell, 108n
Phoenix, 71
Physiologus, 122
Pigmies, 76
Pisgah, 109
Plato, 65
Pliny, 26, 28, 31, 31n, 32, 36n, 37, 39, 67, 71, 76n, 92, 99, 103, 115n, 121, 137, 139; strange tales, 88, 140
Plutarch, 23, 93, 111
Polo, Marco, 55, 135
Pontus (Black Sea), 51, 134, 137
Pope, E. M., 24n
Portuguese, 44; trade in Africa, 16n
Pory, John, translator of Leo, 114
Prester John, 15
Proserpina, 6, 108, 139
Ptolemy, 12, 26, 73, 122, 136, 139
Pulci, 95
Punjab, 13
Purchas, Samuel, 5, 7, 15, 16, 19n, 20n, 23, 36n, 42, 43, 46, 47, 48, 50, 51-52, 52, 58, 58n, 59, 59n, 64, 68n, 69, 70, 70n, 78, 82, 85, 89n, 91n, 95n, 96, 96-101, 103n, 111, 111-112, 112, 114n, 115, 115n, 116, 116n, 117, 126, 126n, 131, 135, 136; used extensively in writing of History of Moscovia, 47, 59, 64, 97
Pursglove, William, 59
Pythian Vale, 82

Quiloa, 15, 16, 16n, 98, 140

Ralegh, Sir Walter, 20n, 21n, 23, 32n, 36n, 101n, 103n, 108n, 111, 112n, 115n, 118, 120, 126, 136; Milton's use of his History of the World, 20n

Index

Red Sea, 76, 76n
Rhine River, 91, 95, 121
Rimmon, 110, 111
Romans, extent of Roman power, 38; methods of fighting, 40
Rome, 65, 119, 127, 128
Russia, 3, 6, 15, 29n, 42 ff., 73, 84, 86, 88, 126, 135; English trade relations with, 42, 42n, 43, 44, 44n, 48; Milton's opinion of it, 42, 44, 45; trade route to discovered by the north, 44, 44n, 56, 88-89; English opinion of the North, 45, 45n; fighting with Tartars, 52, 52n, 53, 54, 54n, 55, 116, 117, 131

Salmasius, 87, 124
Samarchand, 12, 12n, 22, 89, 89n, 96, 125
Samoedia, 47, 50, 81, 130
Samos, 126
Sandys, George, 5, 7, 67n, 78, 102-108, 109n, 114, 115, 118, 119, 128, 139, 140; his *Relation of a Journey* popular, 66, 102, 117; on lack of rain in Egypt, 66; on pyramids, 67; retells classical stories, 102, 107, 108
Satan, 4, 24, 38, 50n, 51, 53, 55, 60, 61, 61n, 63, 64n, 68, 75, 79, 80, 82, 90, 92, 94, 118, 125, 129, 131, 132, 134; compared to whale, 50n, 122, 128
Scythians, 34, 73; wild incursions, 34
Seaton, Ethel, 68-69, 72
Sejanus, 119
Seleucia (the great), 27, 32, 33, 39
Serbonian bog, 105-106, 115n
Sericana, 91, 125, 127
Shah Abbas, 134
Shakespeare, 23, 68, 93
Shalmaneser, 28, 28n, 29, 29n, 38, 96
Shusky, 42n, 50

Siberia, 45, 47, 51, 126
Sibma, 111
Sicily, 76, 103, 114; Trinacria, 114
Sideris, River, 36n
Sidney, Henry, 62
Sierra Leone, 96, 136, 137
Sin, 50, 57, 59, 86, 107, 130
Sinai, 101
Smith, Sir Thomas, his account of Russia, 43
Snorri Sturlason, 80n
Socrates, 128
Sodom, 118
Sofala, 15, 16, 16n, 135; thought to be Ophir, 15, 16, 97-98, 120
Sogdiana, 26, 34
Solinus, 121
Solomon, and Ophir, 16, 98, 120
Spain, 73, 74, 126n
Spaniards, 20, 20n, 21, 44, 65, 74, 136; tyranny over Indians, 74, 126n
Speed, John, 87-88, 91n
Spenser, Edmund, 21n, 49n, 53, 54, 64n, 65, 73, 82, 116n
Strabo, 28n, 34n, 36, 137, 139
Sugden, E. H., vii, 76n, 81n, 82n
Sultan, 15n, 93, 129; "Turchestan-born," 80
Sumatra, 86, 126, 127
Sus, 17, 18, 18n, 114
Susa, 30, 31, 31n, 107, 126
Susiana, 26, 28n, 31, 36, 37
Syene, 76, 76n, 139
Syria, 33, 34, 110, 134
Syrtis, 76

Tacitus, 37
Tagus, 73
Tamburlaine, 12, 89
Taprobane, probably Sumatra, 127, 131
Tarshish, 76n, 126
Tarsus, 76, 76n, 126
Tartaria, 94

Index

Tartars, 29n, 35n, 50, 52, 52n, 53, 54, 81, 117, 131; deceptiveness, 55, 55n; method of fighting, 53, 55, 55n, 116, 116n
Tasso, 49n, 140
Tauris, 14, 15, 93, 100
Taurus Mountains, 90, 140
Taylor, Isaac, 90n
Tenerife, Mount, 79, 80; reputation for great height, 79-80, 92, 132, 133
Ten Tribes, led into captivity, 28, 29, 29n
Teredon, 27, 30, 32, 32n, 33, 36, 36n
Ternate, 95, 95n, 116; importance in trade, 95, 132
Terrestrial Paradise, 69-70, 89, 120, 129, 138
Thessalian witch, 81
Thompson, E. N. S., 17n, 51n, 72n, 99, 106n, 109n
Tiberius, 119
Tidore, 95, 95n, 116; importance in trade, 95, 132
Tigris River, 27, 27n, 77
Tihany, L. C., 54
Todd, H. J., 26n, 31n, 36n, 69, 70n, 94, 97n, 108
Trachinian cliff, 73
Tremisen, 17, 19, 93, 114
Trinity Mss., 10n
Troy, 66
Tunis, 18n
Turkestan, 15n; thought by some to be origin of Turks, 15n, 80, 93
Turkey, 15, 136
Turks, 15n, 93, 128, 129, 129n, 131n; tyranny, 74, 129, 129n

Ultima Thule, 51, 73
Ur, question of location, 77, 93, 113

Vallombrosa, 127
Vardanes, 33
Varthema, 78n
Vasilowich, Ivan, 44, 52
Veer, Gerrit de, 43, 47
Venice, 79
Verity, A. W., 13, 13n, 16n, 18n, 19, 48, 49n, 51n, 54, 67n, 68, 71, 72, 76n, 77, 79, 91, 93, 94, 95, 96, 102, 103, 103n, 105, 106n, 108, 109, 118, 121, 124, 125, 128, 136
Vesuvius, 75, 76, 127-128
Virgil, 36n, 65, 82, 127, 136
Vives, 111
Volga, River, 48, 53, 54
Vologda, 48
Vulgate, 29n

Warner, William, 51
Warton, Thomas, 99, 103n
Whiting, G. W., 15, 26, 28, 32n, 36n, 69, 70n, 72n, 89n, 90, 94, 96n, 99, 102n, 103n, 106n, 108, 108n, 109, 110, 111, 112n, 113, 115n, 123, 127n
Willoughby, Sir Hugh, 44, 47, 62n; great English hero, 44, 56, 60-62; attempt to discover northeast passage, 44

Xenophon, 30
Xerxes, bridging Hellespont, 107, 118, 119, 139

Young, Thomas, 65